HERB
Gardening

HERB
Gardening

Linda Gray

THE CROWOOD PRESS

First published in 2009 by
The Crowood Press Ltd
Ramsbury, Marlborough
Wiltshire SN8 2HR

www.crowood.com

British Library Cataloguing-in-Publication Data
A catalogue record for this book is available from the British Library.

ISBN 978 1 84797 115 9

Illustrations by Charlotte Kelly.

DEDICATION
To the pure magic of nature!

Disclaimer
The authors and the publisher do not accept responsibility, or liability, in any manner whatsoever for any error or omission, nor any loss, damage, injury, or adverse outcome of any kind incurred as a result of the use of the information contained in this book, or reliance upon it.

Typeset by Servis Filmsetting Ltd, Stockport, Cheshire
Printed and bound in Malaysia by Times Offset (M) Sdn Bhd

Contents

Introduction

Herbs have been an important part of the garden for many years. Not only are they full of nutritious vitamins and minerals, they are also full of surprises. *Herb Gardening* aims to transform the mystery of herbs into an everyday gardener's magic. With methods of propagation, cultivation and a little insight into the magic, growing herbs becomes a wonderful and fulfilling experience.

Although we imagine most plants to be ready for use during the late summer to autumn months, many herbs will come to maturity at other times of the year, and some can be grown inside and out, all year round.

Before starting your herb garden, whether it is outside, in a greenhouse or on a windowsill, read through the requirements of each herb in this book to get the best results.

During the early spring, most of us have a natural urge to rush into the garden, dig away until we get backache and plant lots of flower and vegetable seeds. A little forward planning can not only save the aching back but will also get far better results than randomly planting anything and everything.

To begin, consider the space you have available and make a few plans on paper. List the herbs you like to use and include those that create a wonderful ambiance in your garden, either with their smell, foliage, flowers or all three.

In Chapter One, you will find a few ideas for designing your herb garden. Herbs can also be grown in containers, as well as indoors. Chapters Two and Three suggest why you should choose these methods and the best way of going about them. Further advice on cultivation is given in Chapter Four.

Refer to the individual herbs in Chapters Five and Six for planting and harvesting times, as well as detailed growing recommendations.

Gardening with herbs is probably the easiest and often the most delicious garden chore. *Herb Gardening* will help you get the most out of your herb garden.

CHAPTER 1

Designing a Herb Garden

The traditional English herb garden.

The only limitation you have when designing a beautiful herb garden is your imagination! There are so many designs you can adopt, depending on the amount of space, time and energy you have available; and to some extent, budget. Start with something simple if you're starting from scratch or are limited for space. A herb garden can grow and be added to, and will mature over the years with fairly little maintenance.

Decide what you want to grow. A stroll around the garden often helps stimulate ideas, or just imagine what herbs you bought to add to dinner last night. Many cooks like to grow the spaghetti herbs; mainly oregano, parsley and garlic. Or you may prefer to grow a selection of herbs to complement roast dinners, or casseroles.

As well as culinary herbs, there are the aromatic ones that make your home smell fresh, like lavender, mint and basil. These herbs can be dried and used in pot pourri mixtures, or picked fresh from the garden and displayed in a vase or bowl. Mix a few fresh sprigs of lavender in a vase of unscented or dried flowers.

There are a number of herbs that any amateur herbalist can grow to treat minor ailments; for example thyme, mint and parsley are all good digestive aids.

There are also the ornamentals that enhance a flowerbed, as well as being useful in other ways. Lavender and marigolds look spectacular and are also useful in culinary and medicinal preparations.

PLANTING

Before you plant your herbs, check how big they are likely to grow. Allow enough space around each plant for it to fully develop. You should also consider height; don't plant taller growing herbs where they will shade other plants in the garden.

Aromatic and beautiful, lavender is an essential in any herb garden.

Get to know your garden. Work out the hot spots and the shady parts before planting anything, and check for any wind tunnels or frost pockets. The more you know about the space that you are using, the better it will be for your herbs. Position them in a sheltered spot, a sunny, or partially shaded area according to their individual needs.

The soil must be well drained to grow herbs successfully. If your ground is a little heavy, dig in some sand before planting. Herbs rarely need well-fertilized soil to thrive. Too much fertilizer will encourage lots of foliage, but the strength of taste or scent will be reduced. Only a few herbs benefit from extra feeding. These are often the ones that are high in mineral content. Parsley is a good example of a herb that welcomes a rich soil.

DESIGNS

A herb bed in a circular design is very effective and, with a few attractive rocks, bricks or very low fencing, you can easily create a stunning herb garden that will last many years. A cartwheel design is fairly easy to produce and even better if you can pick up an authentic cartwheel from a farmer's auction.

Draw out your plan first and collect the materials you need to complete the job, if you can. But, as long as the growing spots are left undisturbed, all other edgings, pathways, trellises and decorations can be added later. Include in your sketch all the herbs you want to plant and where. Decide what to plant between the spokes if you have a cartwheel design in mind. Colour can be incorporated, and flowering herbs can be planted together, or as a centrepiece with evergreen herbs around them.

Circles and curves are always good focal points in a garden, but there is no reason why you can't produce squares or triangles, or get creative and design a patchwork-style courtyard with herbs arranged according to colour and flowering displays. A new area of paving, bricks or cobbles can be designed with small beds for your herbs. Draw out a plan and decide where the growing spots should be. Leave these areas unpaved, fill with a potting compost or topsoil and plant the herbs.

Having narrow paths around the beds enables easy access for maintaining your plants. Wherever

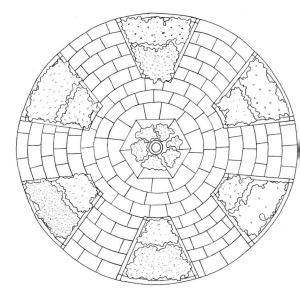

A circular design for a herb garden.

you plant your herbs, you need to have easy access to them or they will be forgotten. Paving saves you having to put your wellies on every time you want a sprig of parsley! Or let your herbs spread over rocks.

A large herb bed can be a centrepiece to your garden, while smaller patches of herbs dotted around will enhance flowerbeds or cheer up the vegetable garden; or simply use them to brighten up a dull spot. Liven up a vast expanse of lawn with a selection of herbs and flowers inset into beds. If the family want to play tennis, create a wonderful herb border round the lawn. Position your herbs so that some are flowering in different borders at different times of the year. Marigolds are great to plant around a lawn area. The bright yellow and orange flowers bloom from mid-summer to autumn, and will last until the first frost of the winter. If all else fails, marigolds will come to the rescue!

A difficult corner can be utilized as a herb garden. There are a number of herbs, including the popular mint family, which will thrive in a semi-shady spot. Taller herbs grow up into the light and don't always need a sunny spot to thrive. All plants will need a certain amount of light, so it's doubtful any herbs will grow successfully behind the shed.

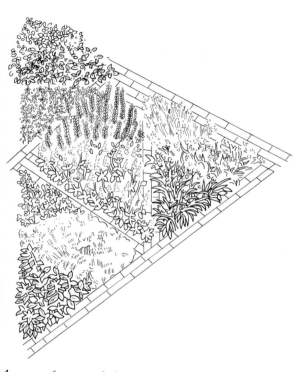

A corner of a square bed can be used for herbs.

...out semi or dapple-shaded areas will be fine for ...ome herbs.

The most well known culinary and medicinal herbs that will tolerate semi-shade are:

- Chives
- Comfrey
- Mint
- Nettles
- Sage
- Thyme

HERBS AND VEGETABLES

...he French invented the potager to get the most ...rowing area out of a small space. They planted ...erbs with fruits and vegetables in small uniformed ...eds. Herbs grow well with vegetable crops as many ...f them are strong smelling and deter pests and flies ...om your crops.

Small, uniformly shaped vegetable beds are easy ...o maintain in a large or small garden. Plant herbs

around the edges of these beds to provide colour, pest deterrents, or for culinary and medicinal use.

- Growing basil with the tomatoes is a must – basil is known as the 'tomato herb' and should always be served with tomatoes to enhance their flavour. Both tomatoes and basil are annual plants.
- Plant nasturtiums thickly around a bed of leeks. The shade they provide will blanch the leeks, that would otherwise need earthing up. This leaves one less job to do.
- Marigolds deter white fly from your asparagus and look stunning in the vegetable garden! They also encourage bees. Plant a few in all the fruit and vegetable growing areas.
- Curly or flat-leaved parsley grown around a red cabbage patch is how we all imagine our vegetable gardens should look!

There are a number of good and bad companion-planting tips you could try in the garden. Certain herbs and vegetables will grow well together. Herbs can be easily planted among the vegetables, and most herbs deter pests because of their strong scent. *See* the section on companion planting in Chapter Four for an idea of how to pair up your herbs and vegetables.

In a potager garden, herbs and vegetables are combined.

SEATS AND PATHS

A favourite way to grow herbs is alongside a path – brushing against the aromatic foliage and flowers releases the scent and produces a true sense of well-being for everyone in the surrounding area. Grow a lavender shrub next to a garden seat or close to an arbour. Positioning your herbs around seating areas, or along pathways, gives friends and family a chance to enjoy them and keeps the herbs firmly in mind at dinnertime.

Herbs on or around a patio area make an excellent talking point, and can encourage children and adults to try different tastes and enjoy the smells.

An old-fashioned brick path is a perfect place to grow thyme and other aromatic herbs. Plant the herbs close to the edge and let them sprawl over the path a little. When the leaves are walked on, the scent is released.

FORMAL DESIGNS

Dwarf box hedges can be incorporated into a geometric design, using hedging in place of rock or wooden dividers. The hedges will need to be kept trimmed and care should be taken to ensure that the hedge does not shade sun-loving plants. A living and growing boundary needs more maintenance, but if you have the time, the inclination, or an enthusiastic garden helper to do the job, then it is well worth the trouble.

Many of the country estate gardens in Britain had box hedging in their formal garden designs, along with an army of gardeners on constant alert with their shears. Low nesting birds can cause a problem if you are sowing herb seed directly on site, but most herbs can be started in a seedbed and transplanted.

Choose an evergreen hedge that grows well in your region. Laurel can be an alternative to privet-type hedges. Keep cutting, and laurel will grow thick and fast, and it is easy to maintain. The deep-coloured, shiny leaves make an attractive border to a herb garden.

An alternative to hedging is a miniature wooden fence. There are sections of decorative edging available at most garden suppliers. Or make one yourself!

WALLED BEDS

Walled raised beds make beautiful herb gardens and are much easier to tend than lower growing herbs. Raised beds are helpful for avoiding back and knee problems, as well as being practical for physically challenged gardeners. An added bonus is that the higher the beds are built, the less the weeds seem to take hold.

The walled garden should be permanent, or near-permanent, therefore position and size must be considered carefully before the job of building gets underway. Materials need to be bought, and possibly a builder employed to do the job.

Choose the sunniest spot you can. Although some shade is good for many herbs, there is usually a shady spot in the garden that is crying out to be filled with a useful plant. Use that spot to grow your mint or other shade-loving plants and build your raised beds in the sun!

Raised walled beds are usually built in a trough design with higher sides. This works well as long as there is good drainage. However large the container is, the confined soil, with little drainage for water, will deteriorate rapidly. All plants need drainage, and few will thrive in waterlogged conditions, so whatever structure you are designing for your herb garden, drainage should be priority. In a walled bed, at least 60cm (2ft) high, there shouldn't be any need to create a solid bottom to the trough shape. The walls will do the job of containing your herbs.

As well as geometric designs, raised beds, patio and pathway displays, herbs can also be grown in

A raised bed.

Brick paths are useful for containing herbs as well as allowing access.

- Most herbs can be placed amongst the flowers in your garden as well as with the fruit and vegetable plots.
- Try planting herbs around a lawned area. Relaxing on a warm summer's day with the smell of aromatic herbs and the sound of bees buzzing is probably one of the most relaxing things you can enjoy, especially after a hard week of work.

As with flowers and vegetables, it is important to plant your herbs in the right places. Taller growing plants have to be planted at the back of a bed so they don't shade the lower growing plants. Some will be very invasive, such as mint, and will take over a whole bed in no time if not contained. Mint does quite well though in a shady area, so can be used to fill a space where other plants struggle to survive.

a simple bed wherever you have the space, as long as it is not too shady. Choose a fairly sunny spot and keep the beds fairly narrow, or create a path so you won't tread down the soil when tending your plants. This could be a few broken paving slabs or anything natural that you can walk on without slipping. Old house bricks cemented together can make a practical edge to your herb and flowerbeds.

RANDOM PLANTING

Herbs are wonderful for planting amongst your flowers or vegetables and will encourage bees for pollination. The vegetable garden is the perfect place to have herbs dotted about. Growing basil amongst your tomatoes is a must and coriander will deter a number of bugs from your vegetable crops. Nasturtiums grow well in the vegetable plot, although they do spread. Plant them around the edges so their growth can be controlled.

- Allow a patch of mint to take over a shady spot by the kitchen door, and always have fresh mint sauce available in the kitchen.
- A bunch of chives can be placed in odd corners around the garden, with the vegetables, herbs or flowers. They look fresh and green for most of the year and produce wonderful bright flowers. Chive flowers can be mixed into a bowl of salad or used to garnish many dishes.

Mint can be useful in shady parts of the garden.

Careful thought and planning before you begin planting your herbs can result in a stunning display that will last for many years.

Annual herbs, such as basil will need starting every year but others last two or more years. Rosemary will thrive in the right conditions for twenty years before it needs replacing and sage grows well for four or five years. A little maintenance will keep herbs thriving. One way to keep your herbs healthy and thriving is to use them! Remember to pick them regularly and they will re-grow quickly.

DESIGNING TO A THEME

As well as the shape of the growing areas and positioning of your plants, herb gardens can also be designed with a particular theme in mind.

Pot-pourri herbs

Create a whole bed of herbs to use in pot-pourri in the house. Choose strongly scented ones such as lavender, mint, and roses. A well-placed citrus tree will add density to the scent of the other herbs, as well as providing lemon or lime fruits later on. Collect your chosen leaves and/or flowers and dry

Pot-pourri.

them. Display in a decorative pot-pourri dish. Dried lavender flowers can be sewn into muslin bags and placed between clothes in a drawer or hung in the wardrobe.

A forest of herbs

A dense collection of leafy herbs planted in a shady corner of the garden will brighten up an otherwise boring spot. Place a common elder in the darkest corner and spread mints and lemon balm around and in front for good ground cover. Many herbs will grow in shady conditions, as long as the ground is well drained and the plants get a fair amount of light, even if they don't get very much direct sun.

When designing to a theme, you can step out of the everyday herb varieties, and go for variegated types. New hybrid herbs can be found in most nurseries and garden suppliers. Look for red and orange tinted or patterned leaves to really enhance the forest effect.

Butterfly garden

There are a number of herbs that attract butterflies. Plant a selection to encourage the wildlife into your garden. Butterflies are attracted to creeping thyme, dill, sage, mint, oregano and parsley. A butterfly herb garden can be large or small, but a quiet spot in the garden will encourage more wildlife in general.

Make a shallow puddle near your herbs to really make the butterflies feel at home.

Colour

Colour schemes are fun to work with in the garden, whether you are growing herbs, flowers or a mixture of both. A silvery design is easy to create using lavenders, rosemary and thyme varieties. Or you could experiment with shades of green foliage or different coloured flowers. Chives, sage and rosemary all produce purple-blue flowers, while nasturtiums are brightly coloured and will brighten up a very green patch. Nasturtiums trail and are good for ground cover, but if you don't need the ground cover buy a variety that climbs and trail it along a fence or trellis behind your smaller plants.

Herb colours.

Kitchen herbs.

Because herbs are generally good companion plants, they can be grown among the flowerbeds as well as on their own. An oregano or thyme border brings all the colours in your flowerbed to life, while marigolds are a herb gardener's best friend. They are a practical flower to grow – they help deter pests, and are bright and cheerful to look at. Plant as many as you dare!

Evergreen herbal shrubs set off a rose garden beautifully. If you are starting from scratch and are about to plant a rose garden, consider growing evergreen shrubs in between the rose bushes. Lavender, rosemary and sage are low maintenance herbs and look beautiful with roses.

Experiment with colours and put together what looks pleasing to your eye. Oregano grown round a bed of red-tinged lettuce must be seen! Look for contrasts; lavender growing with lush foliage, geraniums in pots with thyme. Or match your herbs to the patio décor either using colour and/or delicacy or density of the plants.

A garden shed is essential for keeping tools and equipment in.

Culinary

This bed should be ideally situated near the kitchen, or as near to the house as possible, and should include all the herbs you like to use in everyday cooking. Parsley, sage, rosemary and thyme are common favourites, but also include mint, basil and chives if you have the space. Create a cheerful design with your containers and any small piece of ground you can utilize for a kitchen herb garden. Even if you are growing herbs elsewhere in the garden, it's still a good idea to have a few near the kitchen.

Containers

Many herbs can be grown in containers in or out of doors, and can be incorporated into your herb garden design. Use a large container as a centrepiece, smaller ones on corners, or cluster lots of contain-

ers and pots together to form their own display. *See the next chapter for container ideas.*

TOOLS AND EQUIPMENT

The garden shed

The main piece of equipment you need in the garden is a shed to keep tools in. It doesn't have to be huge but it should be big enough for a lawn mower if you need one and a variety of other tools. A shelf or two for pots and small tools will be invaluable.

Place the shed on a hard standing and protect from the elements by painting or preserving the wood. There are organic preservatives on the market these days. The investment is worth it, especially if you live in a fairly wet region.

Position the shed in a place where:

- it won't shade the vegetable plot
- foliage can be trimmed back all around it
- it won't take up a valuable sunny spot.

So all in all, the shed should be allocated a quiet corner of the garden. But it will do its job well there.

Greenhouse

Greenhouses can be dramatic, huge, summerhouse-type constructions or small upright cupboards, with many variations in between. It isn't absolutely necessary to have a greenhouse when you begin gardening, but they are so useful, it will be hard to resist eventually. For bringing on a few seeds a small mini-greenhouse positioned in a sheltered but sunny spot should suffice. Larger greenhouses are useful for growing grapes and tomatoes in cold or wet climates. Also, if you want to experiment with a few exotic plants, a warm greenhouse is perfect. Consider space, position and budget before buying.

To begin cultivating your garden, you will need a range of tools, but these can be kept to a minimum depending on how much physical work you can put in, and how much cash is available.

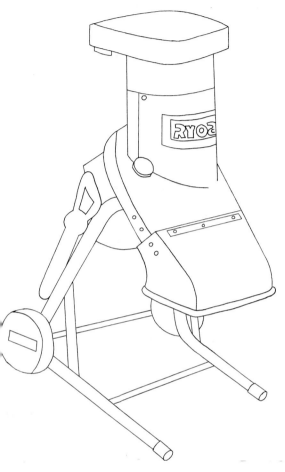

garden shredder.

Machinery

A lawn mower is a must if you have any grassed areas, and a pair of shears and a trimmer would come in handy. It does depend on how much grass needs to be cut and how often you can cut it. A decent lawn mower will serve you well, though – have a good look around before you buy one. They are available in a wide range of sizes and blade adjustments, as well as a choice between petrol-powered or electricity. The choice is yours, but it's worth a little research before you buy.

A rotivator is a wonderful machine for quickly turning up the soil to a depth ready for planting. However, they do require a little practise to use. A rotivator should never be used when the ground is too wet. The blades will clog up and also ruin the consistency of your soil. This is a tool to use when the ground has dried out a little after the winter.

For turning the ground, a spade and fork will do the job just as well. Some traditional gardeners would argue that hand tools are much better as they don't use any electricity or petrol. They are less expensive and sometimes there can be a case of overkill when using machinery. A machine can change the structure of your soil and you may find drainage is affected through the structural change. Used carefully, though, a machine will certainly get the job done faster, so as well as a decent lawn mower, a rotivator may be useful to you, especially if you have a large area to be dug over.

A garden shredder is a handy tool if you have trees or large hedges and shrubs that are pruned regularly. A garden shredder will chew up all your branches up to approximately 4cm (1.5in) diameter, and leave you with plenty of mulch for the garden.

NB: Before you mulch, make sure the wood isn't too acidic. Oak, for example, takes acid from the soil and acid is therefore present in the wood. A cabbage patch prefers an alkali soil and will not thrive with an acidic mulch.

Manual tools

Manual tools are always needed in the garden, and it won't be long before the absolute need for a rake will have you rushing to the garden centre. Start off with a few basics such as a spade, a fork, a rake and a hoe. Then buy a small hand trowel, a pair of comfortable, sturdy gardening gloves and a good pair of secateurs.

A sharp edge on a spade is a must-have for:

- tidying edges of lawned areas
- cutting a clean straight edge around the vegetable plot
- digging over a new plot
- everyday use.

Make sure the spade is a good weight and the handle is the right length for you. Buy a strong, well-made spade as cheaply produced tools can cause accidents.

A selection of small tools that will prove useful for herb gardening.

Make sure the larger tools are the right height and weight for you before you buy. Gardening is physically challenging enough, without using tools that are too heavy or awkward. Using the right tools for the right job can save many a gardening backache.

Choose a fork, rake and a hoe with the same care. The hoe should have a fairly sharp edge the same as a spade. A pair of shears is useful for edging beds and clipping straggly branches from shrubs or small trees.

Buy a good quality trowel, a strong pair of secateurs and some sturdy comfortable gardening gloves and you will be ready to tackle most everyday jobs in the garden.

Clothing

Always wear protective clothing in the garden. As well as protective gloves, you need a warm hat for cold months and a sunhat for the summer months. It's surprising just how much sun you can get in a couple of hours gardening. Sturdy boots are also a must when using machinery or large tools. At other times, a pair of wellies or garden clogs will save you ruining your slippers!

Other equipment

If you are starting from scratch, there will be plent of equipment to acquire, but not all of it needs t be bought. Lots of household items can be recycle to use in the garden

To start all, or some, of your herb and vegetab crops from seed, you will need the following list of garden paraphernalia:

- **Seed trays**: these can be warm propagators spe cially bought or old paint trays, cleaned of all pain and chemicals. As long as the tray is well drained anything that's a couple of inches high and bo shaped will do! A plastic cover that fits over th trays will keep seeds warm on colder nights.
- **Pots of all sizes**: the small square plastic c degradable pots are perfect for potting out toma toes and other plants. Yoghurt and dessert pot well washed and dried work well, but make sur you punch a few holes in the bottom for drain age. A few ordinary plastic and clay pots shoul be acquired as well.
- **Bags of seed and potting compost**: if yo aren't making your own. Sieve home-made com post before use to remove any un-rotted materia and large stones. Otherwise, buy organic com post where possible.
- **Gravel**: collect some stones or gravel for drain age. Put a layer of stones in the bottom of tray and pots before filling with compost.
- **A few clear plastic covers**: these can rang from cloches for large patches of seed in the gar den to smaller individual covers. A plastic wate bottle, cut in half, will keep two small plant warm at night.
- **Row markers**: plastic or wooden ice lolly stick will do the job of marking rows in small see trays and pots, but larger markers will be neede outside. As long as you can write the name o your plants on the marker, it doesn't matter wha you use. A small twig with a paper flag tape round the top will last a while, although the rai may wash off the paper flag fairly quickly.
- **Garden twine**: choose a degradable twine rathe than plastic string that stays around the garde for years. Twine is needed to support tomatoe and other plants.

garden journal is a useful reference tool.

Watering cans: buy a fine, misting spray-bottle for seeds and small plants, and a larger one with a rosette for all other plants

Garden hose: a watering can is perfect for containers on a patio, but a garden hose is essential for larger areas.

There are plenty of different products, gadgets and other paraphernalia available from garden suppliers, but the above list should be enough to get moving with your garden. All tools and equipment should be put away in the shed at the end of each gardening day. Overnight rain will damage metal tools and wooden trays.

Buy a garden journal, or make your own, to note dates of sowings and plantings. Leave a space for comments. It's not necessary to write every detail down, but a few notes can help diagnose problems if they occur. For example, if you know that your green pepper seeds were sown at the end of February but their growth was stunted, you can try planting a little later next year. Make a note of any plant diseases in the garden, and avoid planting vulnerable crops in that area. Similarly, note the results of any treatments and fertilizers used.

One last gardening tip that many of us overlook is – get the kids involved!

The learning and quality time spent with children in the garden is second to none. Depending on their age, they really can help as well. Scaled down tools are available, and children love to get their hands dirty as well as feel they are using adult tools and doing grown-up stuff. They are also getting fresh air and exercise, and learning about a healthy diet; something we all want to pass on to the next generation.

Teach them what the plants are and what we use them for. The learning curve is enormous as well as being fun, and as none of us could ever possibly know everything about every plant, the grown-ups get to learn as well!

Never let your garden become a chore. If the current layout isn't working, try something else. A garden is a constantly growing and changing place and can be adapted to individual needs and tastes as and when the mood takes you.

CHAPTER 2

Growing Herbs in Containers

Containers are the perfect way to grow herbs if you are short of space in the garden, or don't have a garden at all. They are also a perfect solution to herbs that take over the whole garden if left to their own devices. Herbs can be grown in window boxes, on balconies and in pots on a windowsill. Choose the type of container according to your needs, space available and décor.

Hanging baskets have become very popular in the last few years. Herbs will grow well in hanging baskets and can be displayed along with flowers and even a few vegetable crops.

HANGING BASKETS

Hanging baskets can be spectacular to look at as well as practical if you are using them to grow herbs or salad crops. As a rule, herbs that grow well in containers grow well in hanging baskets. They can be mixed in with flowers or even a small salad crop, such as cutting lettuce. Plant a red-tinged variety with oregano around the edge, and allow the oregano to trail over the sides.

Cherry tomatoes can be grown in baskets or containers, along with spaghetti herbs like basil, oregano and parsley. In a large enough container, all these herbs can be grown with a tomato plant very successfully. The plants need room to grow, so they shouldn't be too overcrowded. Large root systems will use up nutrients in the soil quickly and your plants may need an organic feed from time to time.

With a little planning, hanging baskets can be very easy to maintain, once established, and they can brighten up a dull spot around the house or garden. Fix brackets to a brick wall and decorate

with hanging baskets. Display free-standing containers on the ground, and you'd hardly know the wall was there.

Garden suppliers stock a good selection of hanging baskets and all the materials needed to plant them out.

An open wire basket is the traditional base to use. The wire basket needs lining before filling with compost. Traditionally, sphagnum moss has been used for lining baskets, but coconut fibre and other mediums work just as well. An old jumper will even contain the compost! Any lining will work as long as

Hanging baskets can be useful for growing herbs where space is limited.

Filling the empty basket.

the compost can't fall through the wire basket. Try lining the wire basket with grass clippings, placing a black plastic liner inside the grass and then filling with compost. The grass will dry out and develop a thatched look. Remember to add a few drainage holes to the plastic liner, and make a few spaces in the linings for plants to be pushed through.

The compost you use in any container should be new, and as nutrient packed as possible. An organic potting compost is ideal. Soil from the garden could be lacking in minerals and nutrients and may inhibit the growth of your plants. Hanging baskets take a little work to get going, so start with the best compost available.

Fill your lined baskets on third to half full, with compost. Trailing plants, which you want to grow through the sides of the basket should be planted at this level. Lay the roots on the surface of the compost and gently push the plant through the wire basket, so it hangs out of the sides. Cover the roots with compost. Further trailing plants can be planted in layers in this way, until about two thirds of the basket is full. Turn the basket around a little after every planting. Add the plants you intend to grow as the centrepiece of your basket, and firm the compost around them. Water well.

There are products that will hold water in the soil and release fertilizers every so often, but if you have a few minutes a day to tend to your plants, none of these products should be necessary.

Water-drip feeds are a good idea for all containers if you are going away during the summer. The secret with hanging baskets is not to let them dry out.

As the year goes on, baskets can look a bit straggly. Revitalize your display by removing dead flowers, weeds, and generally tidying them up regularly. Put new plants in as others die back.

- Design your baskets according to your tastes and needs – plant out a spicy basket, with a chilli pepper plant and nasturtiums, then add thyme and oregano to trail down the sides.
- Or grow a salad basket with cutting lettuce, basil, thyme and parsley. Design your baskets with colour in mind as well as flavour. A basket of geraniums with nasturtiums trailing around it is attractive in the garden and useful in the kitchen. Although you can't eat geraniums, as far as I know, they make lovely posies for around the house. Plus the fact that nasturtiums are always a useful herb to grow.

Hang the baskets where they are easily accessible and can be used when required. Herbal baskets are better hanging near the kitchen but really can brighten up any area of the garden. Hang one from a tree in a shady spot, and grow shade-loving herbs, such as mint.

WINDOW BOXES

A window box, planted out with the right herbs, can stay green practically all year round, and can be used to decorate the outside of your house at both the front and back. Window boxes have been used as containers for flowers, herbs and vegetables for generations. In recent years, with ornate containers and pots being freely available, they have been slightly overlooked.

A window box must be firmly fixed with no danger of it falling. This is even more important when they are on an upstairs windowsill.

Before buying or making a window box, be sure of the measurements. A box that spans the whole width of a window looks better and will fit in more plants than a shorter one. Secure to the wall with

A windowbox is another solution for the home with little or no garden.

sturdy brackets. A simple, trough-shaped container can also be used on a windowsill.

A very cold side of a building may not be a good site for a window box. Although there are some plants that will cope with wet and windy weather, there are more that like a little sun and shelter. If you are unsure, keep a couple of containers of herbs or other plants at ground level on each side of the house for a season, and gauge the growing conditions.

The same growing rules apply to window boxes as to any container growing:

  must have good drainage
  water daily unless it rains
  use new compost to start and renew every few
  years
  keep weed-free
  remove dead foliage and blooms regularly.

A window box outside the kitchen can be planted out with salad plants and herbs all year round. Position your plants in a zigzag line or randomly, rather than in straight lines. Start off a short line or two of seed (if well protected from the cold) then transplant within the box or elsewhere in the garden.

Plant trailing herbs along the outside edge of the window box, so that they cascade down over the wall of your house. Mix in a few flowers and vegetables if you have the space.

OTHER CONTAINERS

Herbs grown in containers are very effective to look at and are practical – especially when filled with plants that need taking indoors during colder months. The types of containers available are varied, and can be personalized, designed with a theme in mind, or scattered around the garden randomly. Even on a low budget a stunning display can be achieved.

DIY

An old pot that has seen better days doesn't encourage much tender loving care. But if that is all that is available, decorate the pot with a simple painted flower in bright colours or, if you are artistically inclined, let your imagination run wild and create a masterpiece.

Use enamel paints so they last longer and brush a sealing fluid over the whole thing to keep it looking fresh and easier to clean.

This is a perfect moment to get the kids involved! Let them decorate their own pots – even if they are too young to use enamel paints, they can design and paint their pots and you can seal them afterwards with a sealing varnish. This is a real way to get youngsters interested in growing their own plants and encourages them to try out new tastes.

You can decorate your own pots for growing herbs in.

Containers all need to be placed in a dish or a saucer if the pot is small enough. Try and match the dish with the pot.

Use a stand to rest the container on outside or indoors. If you are doing it yourself, simply stand the container on a couple of old clay tiles or small batons of wood. Check wooden batons from time to time, especially if your containers are outside. They will rot through eventually and have to be replaced.

Second-hand

Look out for containers in out-of-the-way places, such as car boot sales, markets and second-hand shops. A collection of random pots on a balcony or patio is very attractive, especially if they all have a story attached. Clay pots tend to dry out very quickly but look wonderful.

Seek out old-fashioned pots, urns or even cauldrons. They can all be used to plant herbs in. Plant out a few summer herbs in a traditional urn or cauldron and you have an instant talking point on the patio. Searching for containers and pots can become addictive though. I have a friend who has hundreds and although every one tells a story, and they look stunning when planted out, they also have to be looked after and maintained. Don't let your containers become a chore.

Pick up a school art sink, or an old-fashioned kitchen sink, and fill with colourful pebbles and seashells. Then place a few pots of herbs in the pebbles. Use decorative pots to make the display even more eye-catching.

A good way to use up bottomless buckets or other old containers is to sink them into the garden. Dig a large enough hole and position the bucket then fill with a mix of soil and potting compost to plant your herbs in. This is a great idea for showing off herbs that grow in out of the way places, where you may not want to use a favourite pot or tub. Also, it will curb the prolifically growing herbs from taking over the garden.

If you have the space, keep a few everyday herbs in pots outside your back door, or as close to the kitchen as possible. Herbs do prefer to be used rather forgotten about!

New containers

The containers you use for your herbs must have sufficient drainage holes in the bottom. If you choose to use a container without drainage, plant your herbs in a pot first and then place the pot into

If you have the space, keep a few everyday herbs in pots outside your back door.

GOOD HERBS FOR CONTAINER GROWING

Many herbs lend themselves to container growing but some are a must!

- Basil grows well in pots on a windowsill or patio.
- Bay prefers a container that doesn't allow it too much growth. It is happy to grow outside but bring it in during a cold winter.
- Chives are perfect on a windowsill or outside.
- Coriander is fine in containers but can re-seed itself given enough space.
- Mint has to be contained. It can be grown in a bucket sunk in the ground, or in a decorative container, but it must be contained!
- Oregano's bright cheerful foliage mixes well with other plants.
- Parsley is grown annually, so it will always be available for cooking.
- Thyme thrives in fairly dry sunny spots.

Purpose-built plant containers often have stands sold with them, usually three small wedges of china or clay that you sit the container on. They work perfectly and don't leave too many marks on the patio. Some containers have stands built in.

Keep the underneath of your containers fairly clean and you will have fewer problems with nesting bugs and staining.

GENERAL GROWING TIPS FOR CONTAINER HERBS

- Containers must be well drained. Use pieces of stone or other drainage material, and pots must have holes in the bottom.
- All container-grown herbs need watering at least once a day. Keep surface of soil damp, but never too wet.
- An organic feed can be used in moderation, but only if the soil is overused and the herbs are suffering. It may be better to re-plant in a new pot with fresh soil.
- Replace soil when transplanting herbs, using new potting compost.
- Give plants enough space to grow. Bay likes a relatively small container and should be grown on its own, whereas smaller growing herbs will be happy to share a container.
- Never spray your herbs with an insecticide. Find a natural alternative to bug attacks.
- Move the containers around from time to time. This will deter any wildlife making a home in, around or underneath your herbs.
- Keep containers weed-free. Weeds will use up valuable nutrients in contained soil.
- Trim your herbs to shape when they start looking straggly or over-grown.
- Remove dead flowers and foliage regularly.

...d container stand.

...he container. Or use containers that are purpose-built and usually have a dish or tray to sit in. A dish ...r tray is essential if you have your plants indoors ...r on outdoor timber decking. If possible, keep ...he container raised off the ground a little. Water ...tains can be difficult to remove, even from paving ...labs. Change the pots around from time to time to ...reshen up the area and create a new display.

CHAPTER 3

Growing Herbs Indoors

Growing herbs indoors creates a fresh atmosphere in your home and, as an added bonus, the plants help keep dust to a minimum. As long as your herbs get plenty of light and air circulation there's no reason why they shouldn't be just as productive as herbs grown outside.

Some herbs are such prolific growers that they aren't practical to grow indoors, unless you have a conservatory you want to fill quickly. Having said that, a prolific herb such as mint can be contained in a pot without needing a very sunny spot to grow well. However, it does need some light.

The other herbs that are not so practical to grow indoors are the larger growing ones, such as rosemary, lavender and sage. They like to grow into shrubs and hedges in their natural habitat, although bonsai versions can be created. To create miniature herbs, simply keep cutting them back into shape. The plants may need to be replaced every year if their growth is stunted through cutting back, but you may be lucky and keep them going for many years.

Herbs grown for the roots, such as horseradish and fennel, are nearly always better outside. Horseradish needs deep soil to develop the root and may not be able to absorb enough nutrients from the soil in a container to keep it thriving, even if the container is fairly deep. Fennel needs earthing up and if kept in a container the same nutrient problem can occur. Fennel, grown for its foliage only, can be grown indoors but it often grows very tall and is not necessarily attractive as an indoor plant. Fennel is best grown outside where it can attract butterflies to the garden.

POSITION

Where you grow your herbs indoors depends on a number of factors.

- Herbs must have good air circulation but shouldn't be positioned in a very draughty cold spot.
- They need light, but not too much direct sunlight through glass. Pots may need to be moved away from windows with direct sunlight during the hottest time of the day, to prevent the leaves being scorched.
- Indoors, pots and containers must be placed where they won't be tripped over, knocked or damaged.
- Keep away from direct heat such as radiators and open fires.

Central heating in your home could dry your pots very quickly. Keep an eye on them when you put the radiators back on in the autumn. They may need a little extra light and water.

A collection of herbs grown on a kitchen windowsill is always available for cooking. Open the window on warm days so that the plants get plenty of air circulation.

Popular herbs to grow in a bright kitchen, or on a windowsill, are basil, chives and parsley. Parsley is a biennial and will grow tall before going to seed in its second year of growth. Replace with a fresh pot every year. Basil is an annual and needs to be planted every year. A chive plant could last a number of years, but will need re-potting as the plant gets bigger.

Most herbs can be grown in pots on a windowsill.

POTS AND THINGS

Containers are probably one of the most important pieces of equipment if you want to grow a collection of herbs indoors for display purposes. For practical use, most herbs will grow just as well on a windowsill in a regular plant pot.

In the previous chapter there are many ideas for containers. Beautiful urns and vases, tureens and bowls of all shapes and sizes can be artistically used in an indoor herb display.

If you have the space indoors, or possess a large conservatory, then an old pond lining or paddling pool could serve as a container. It must be rigid and have good drainage, which will mean also having a large enough base to sit it on, or risk ruining the carpets. If the container is large enough, a mix of soil and sand with a layer of gravel may be sufficient drainage. Test before planting your herbs.

Large containers can be planted indoors, just as an outdoor herb garden would be, but in mini-

ature. Have fun with this. Herbs like to be cut and used, and if you cut them to the shape required and look after them well, a miniature herb garden will last for years. Buy compact hybrid varieties if you can. Regular plants may suffer if their growth is continually stunted through over-cutting.

For smaller spaces, look around for pots that will be just right! Charity shops and car boot sales can be a gold mine for containers. Think herb display while you are searching and the right one for you will show up.

Scour the larger garden centres and horticultural shows for interesting pots, troughs or old-fashioned butler sinks, although these may not blend too well with the living room furniture. But then again they might!

Keeping herbs indoors and thriving does require a little attention. Try not to forget about them. It's very easy to see something every day and never really notice that it's screaming for attention. Make the pots attractive so they catch your eye and then you will remember to water them.

Keep an area free for bringing in your pots in winter. A bay tree will grace your patio from spring to autumn, but should be brought indoors during the cold winter months.

STARTING YOUR HERBS

Before planting your herbs, fill the pots and containers with a mixture of sand and potting compost.

Indoor herbs need particularly good drainage and the sand will help. A layer of gravel in the bottom of your pots should also be added for drainage.

Make a plan of:
- what herbs to plant
- what containers to use
- where they will need to be positioned in the house.

A decorated pot can brighten up a windowsill.

The chives you bought may suit Great Aunt Dora's antique emerald cauldron, but the cauldron will not necessarily fit on the windowsill!

Buy small plants from a garden supplier or start your herbs from seed. If you decide to buy your plants ready grown, make sure they look healthy. Plants you buy from a garden supplier will have been grown with plenty of light. At home you may find the light levels are lower and the herbs need to be acclimatized before being used. Keep them in as much light as possible and look after them until they start to produce new leaves. The new leaves are a sign the plant is acclimatized to the new light levels and you can start using your herbs from this point on, but not before.

Seed can be started directly in the containers, although they will need thinning later on. Choose 'compact' varieties of herb seeds, if you can find them, and always check on recommended growing conditions before you buy. Some hybrid varieties may have been developed specifically for outdoor growing or climbing.

Start seeds in seed trays or small pots of compost. When your plants are a few inches tall, re-pot into slightly larger pots or thin out plants started in trays. The thinned-out plants can then be potted on or planted out in the garden, weather permitting. Water regularly but don't over-water. The compost should be kept damp but not wet. There are detailed growing recommendations for forty favourite herbs in Chapters Six and Seven.

GROWING

Your plants will need light and water, although not too much water. In a centrally heated home you should try to keep the plant in a position with good airflow – a bright hallway maybe. The soil should be kept damp but not wet as too much water will deprive your plants of oxygen. Yellowing leaves is a sign of over-watering. Water once every week or two, in the mornings preferably. Any excess water will evaporate during the day. Plants grow less in the winter, if at all and should be watered less often, perhaps only once a month. If the soil feels dry then give the plant water, but never over-water, especially during the winter months.

A fan placed nearby will help improve airflow conditions for all plants.

Indoor plants can't tap into the nutrients deep in the soil as they can outside. It is advisable to feed herbs once every couple of weeks during the growing season, and once a month during the winter. Use an organic fertilizer. This will help keep your plants healthy and thriving.

A fan placed nearby will help improve airflow conditions for all plants, although if windows and doors are regularly opened, this shouldn't be necessary.

During the summer months, put your plants outdoors for an extra boost of sun and air. Bring them in at night, before the temperature drops. Most herbs will flourish in temperatures between 55° and 70°F. Some may cope with slightly lower or higher temperatures, but overall it is doubtful they will grow well.

Six hours of sunlight every day is the ideal environment for most herbs, although mint, rosemary, sage and parsley will cope with less.

A fluorescent light or a specifically designed grow light from a garden supplier can be invaluable in a low-light environment or when the days start getting shorter. Make sure the lights are positioned 15 to 23cm (6 to 9in) above the tops of your plants. Check this height regularly to allow for growth.

Pests don't tend to be a problem indoors, although cats have been known to object to pots on their windowsill and may take to eating your herbs.

At the end of the growing season, the soil in your containers can become compact. Rake over lightly with a small indoor rake to loosen and aerate the soil.

When perennial herbs get too big for their pots, take cuttings or divide the roots (as in chives). Plant the bigger pieces outside or give them away, and re-pot a smaller piece for the windowsill. Choose a young shoot for cuttings and a fresh healthy root if you are propagating by root division. Use new compost for new containers.

WHICH HERBS TO CHOOSE

Larger growing herbs such as sage or rosemary can be kept small enough to grow indoors, but they need clipping regularly to prevent them becoming straggly and overshadowing other herbs. Even lavender will grow inside, but all plants need good air circulation.

Other herbs *not* to grow indoors are: dandelions, daisies, dog rose and blackberry. All these herbs grow outside in most moderate and fairly cold climates and anyway some grow far too big for the average home. At a pinch, thornless blackberries could be grown in a conservatory – but would need plenty of air circulation, and water.

In a bright conservatory most everyday herbs will thrive given the right care and attention. Create a display of shelves with containers of herbs trailing over them or use a large container to grow many different herbs in one place. Decorate with rocks or seashells, or coloured pebbles. Create a herbal masterpiece for your home.

Herbs that grow particularly well indoors are as follows.

- Basil is perfect on a windowsill. It repels flies and a few leaves placed on a hot grill after a barbeque will deter mosquitoes as well.
- Bay can be grown indoors, but only during the cold months. Leave outside on a patio or balcony from spring to autumn.
- Chives are another definite for the windowsill. Keep cutting and using, and re-pot every couple of years into a larger container.
- Mint is happy inside as long as it's not in a very sunny spot. Keep a large pot of mint in the house to freshen the air.
- Oregano likes a bright, sunny position. It is ideal to have available as a culinary herb.
- Thyme also prefers a bright sunny position. It is useful during the winter months for treating cold and flu symptoms, as well as adding to recipes.

CHAPTER 4

Propagation, Cultivation, Pests and Diseases

PROPAGATION

The propagation of herbs can be as simple as throwing a few seeds in a pot and waiting for them to grow. But sometimes they are a bit trickier to get going. There are various ways to get your herbs started: seeds, layering, cuttings or root division are the most usual methods. And of course many herbs are available to buy as small plants from garden suppliers.

Some herbs take so long for the seed to germinate that unless you are an expert or extremely patient, a different approach may be more suitable. Some of the herbs listed in this book are grown from seed, others are more suitable to start from layering, cuttings or root division. Generally, annual plants are grown from seed whilst biennials and perennials are propagated by other methods. The following checklist is a quick glance at the best way of propagating each of the herbs listed.

Seed

Early spring is the usual time to start seeds for annual plants and late spring for biennials. In most

Some of the equipment you will need for propagation.

EVERYDAY HERBS

- **Basil**: seed. The only sure way to get basil going is from seed.
- **Bay**: cuttings or layering. Seed is possible but germination can be poor.
- **Celery**: seed. There is no other way.
- **Chives**: seed or root division from a healthy established plant.
- **Coriander**: seed. It will re-seed itself successfully.
- **Dill**: seed. This herb germinates well generally.
- **Fennel**: seed. Don't mix other seeds in same container.
- **Garlic**: seed. The individual cloves are considered to be seed in this instance.
- **Horseradish**: seed or root division from an established plant.
- **Lavender**: cuttings from a healthy plant.
- **Lemon Balm**: cuttings or root division.
- **Lovage**: seed or root division from an established plant.
- **Marigolds**: seed. Good germination rate.
- **Mint**: seeds or root division. Both work well.
- **Nasturtiums**: seed. They often re-seed themselves.
- **Oregano**: seed. Good germination rate.
- **Parsley**: seed. Seed can be collected during the second year of growth.
- **Rosemary**: cuttings from an established healthy plant.
- **Sage**: cuttings or layering. Seed works but plant needs to grow for a year before using.
- **Thyme**: root division or cuttings. Seed works, but again, the plant needs to grow for a year before using.

OCCASIONAL HERBS

- **Aloe Vera**: seed or root division.
- **Angelica**: seed or root cuttings. Seeds must be sown just after ripening.
- **Blackberry**: cuttings (canes).
- **Borage**: seed. Will re-seed itself in the right environment.
- **Burdock**: seed. Although burdock grows wild in many areas.
- **Caraway**: seed. It will often re-seed itself.
- **Chamomile**: seed. It will normally re-seed itself.
- **Chervil**: seed. Will re-seed itself in the right environment.
- **Comfrey**: root cuttings or pieces of crown of an established plant.
- **Daisy**: seed. It grows wild extensively.
- **Dandelion:** seed. It grows wild extensively.
- **Dog Rose**: seed can take two years to germinate. Layers or cuttings are quicker.
- **Echinacea**: seed. It will re-seed itself; division from older plants only.
- **Feverfew**: seed or cuttings.
- **Savory**: seed or cuttings from winter savory. Seed from summer savory.
- **Sorrel**: Seed. It germinates quickly.
- **Tarragon**: French tarragon from cuttings, Russian tarragon from seed.
- **Violet**: seed or cuttings.
- **Watercress**: seed or cuttings from a bunch of bought watercress.
- **Yarrow:** cuttings or division.

climates, the seeds will need to be kept weed-free, watered and warm. Start them off in a greenhouse, conservatory or on a windowsill. Always start seed in well-drained trays or pots of new potting compost. As long as the seeds get enough light, water and warmth, germination will occur. See individual herbs for watering suggestions, and always check seed packets where applicable for growing recommendations in your region.

Many herb seeds are notoriously difficult to germinate. Try other methods of germination where possible.

Root division, layering and cuttings are usually started in spring or autumn. If a very cold winter is expected wait until the spring, unless you are growing your plants indoors or they can be protected well from frozen ground.

Seed packets.

Root division

Root division is normally done in spring or autumn. If a very cold winter is expected, spring is probably the best time to divide your herbs to give them a chance to become established and settled again throughout the summer months.

Dig up the whole root system carefully with a fork. Dig wide of the stem to minimize damage to the roots. Gently pull roots apart until you have two or more pieces with healthy shoots on each.

Re-plant these pieces as soon as possible after digging up. Choose a similar position in the garden, either in sun, partial sun or shade. Firm down with your heel and water well.

Layering

Layering can be done at most times of the year, although spring and autumn are usually the best times. Only layer from a strong healthy plant. Choose an undamaged lower branch and fix it to the ground with a U-shaped peg, without pulling or putting too much strain on either the branch or the main plant. Cover the pegged area with an inch or so of fresh compost and water gently.

When the branch has produced new roots, probably in the following spring or autumn, cut the branch from the main plant. The new plant can be left to grow alongside the mother plant or moved to a new location. Dig up carefully to avoid damaging the new roots and re-plant immediately.

Cuttings

Cuttings can be taken from many woody-type shrubs including lavender and sage. Cuttings are best started in early spring or autumn. Or try to get some going at any time you decide to trim back your main plants. Choose healthy 8 to 11cm (3 to in) stems, with a 'heel' if possible. Push into well-drained pots of new compost and water well. Keep the compost damp and fairly warm until the stems have produced roots. Some herbs will take as long as a year to become strong enough to re-plant and some may not work at all. For this reason it's best to plant as many as you have space for. Too many better than not enough.

When your cuttings are starting to show signs of life and producing leaf, they can be re-potted or put out into the garden. Plant as you would with any other plant. Firm down and water well. Keep weed free and look after the new plants for the first year until they become established.

CULTIVATION

Cultivating, from seed to harvest, should never be considered a garden chore. Maybe mowing the lawn gets a bit tedious sometimes, but growing your own herbs for decoration, flavourings and medicinal comforts is always an enjoyable experience.

In general plants need light, water and a few nutrients in the soil. If they get these in the right

Blue basil.

combination you have a crop. If the plant doesn't get its requirements, it dies. Thanks to herbalists, gardeners and enthusiastic food growers over the centuries, lots of information has been recorded which we can access to help us grow our herbs and other plants successfully.

THERE ARE THREE MAIN TYPES OF GROWING LIFE FOR PLANTS:

Annuals: planted every year. Examples of everyday annual herbs are:

- **Basil**
- **Celery** – hybrid varieties. Other celery types are biennial.
- **Coriander**
- **Dill**
- **Marigold**
- **Nasturtiums** – in warmer climates can be perennial.

Biennials: plants that last for two years, usually flowering in the second year. Examples of everyday biennial herbs are:

- **Celery** – hybrids are generally annual.
- **Fennel** – also perennial and sometimes cultivated as an annual.
- **Garlic** – also perennial and often cultivated as an annual.
- **Parsley**

Perennials: These will carry on growing year after year, in the right conditions. Examples of everyday perennial herbs are:

- **Bay**
- **Chives**
- **Fennel** – also biennial and sometimes cultivated as an annual.
- **Garlic** – also biennial but usually cultivated as an annual.
- **Horseradish**
- **Lavender**
- **Lemon Balm**
- **Lovage**
- **Mint**
- **Nasturtiums** – only perennial in a warm climate.
- **Oregano**
- **Rosemary**
- **Sage**
- **Thyme**

Herbs are the most wonderfully accommodating plants because they love to be used. Use the herbs regularly and they will produce more foliage and become stronger. Keep all plants weed-free as much as possible, especially in the early stages until they become established. Weeds can strangle new plants and should be removed as soon as they are visible, wherever possible.

Some herbs, such as thyme, thrive in fairly dry conditions and shouldn't be watered too often. In wet climates thyme very rarely needs any extra water. Others, like mint, prefer a damper, less sunny environment, although all herbs, apart from water cress, won't survive their roots being waterlogged. All pots, containers and outside beds should be well-drained at all times.

Mulch

Herbs benefit from mulching in winter months. A fairly thick mulch of lawn or hedge clippings, straw or other organic material will help keep the roots warm and protect them from frost. Care should be taken that the stems get enough air circulation. Mulch close to the plant but allow some space for them to breathe and grow. Herbs that prefer damp, shady areas but find themselves in a sunny dry spot will benefit from mulching as it helps to keep the ground damp.

Feed

Most herbs, with the possible exception of parsley, don't need feeding very often. Too much fertilizer will create too much foliage too quickly. In general your herbs will get enough nutrients from the soil to produce the right amount of foliage. Any more could attract aphids and weaken your plants. Only feed herbs when you are absolutely sure that they need it.

Grow herbs and vegetables together in the garden and the different crops will take and put back nutrients into and from the soil to keep a well-balanced environment for all your plants.

COMPANION PLANTING

Companion planting helps with the maintenance in a garden. Certain plants grow well together and will get along happily without you having to do much.

Single-leaf basil.

Borage in flower.

Single leaves of chives.

Herbs deter many pests because of their strong scent, and other useful components. Here are a few examples of herbs with their good and bad companion.

Basil
Good with tomatoes, peppers and asparagus.
Avoid growing near sage.
Repels many insects, including mosquitoes and flies.
Attracts butterflies.
Grown with chamomile, the essential oil will be stronger.

Borage
Good with almost anything, especially strawberries and squash plants.
A magic herb. Welcome everywhere in the garden.
Repels insects.
Attracts honeybees.

Chives
Good with apples and brassicas (such as cabbage or broccoli) and carrots.

- Avoid growing near peas and beans.
- Repels carrot fly and aphids.

Dill
- Good with cabbages, lettuce and cucumbers.
- Avoid growing with carrots and tomatoes.
- Repels spider mite and aphids.
- Attracts wasps and honeybees.
- It comes from the same family as fennel and is one of the few plants that will grow with fennel. Fennel should be planted away from most other plants in the garden, although it does attract ladybirds.

Dill seed head.

Lovage.

Garlic cloves.

Mint.

Garlic

- Good with cucumbers, apples and pears, lettuce and peas.
- Will grow happily with most plants.
- Repels aphids, ants and rabbits.

Lovage

- Another magic herb, good to grow with almost anything.
- Lovage doesn't like to grow too close to rhubarb.
- Attracts wasps and ground beetles (good bugs).
- Lovage, like borage, is said to improve the health of most plants.

Oregano

- Good to grow alongside many plants, includin tomatoes and peppers.
- Repels aphids.
- Allow to spread around pepper plants for extr humidity.

Mint

- Good to grow with brassicas (including all kal varieties and cabbages).
- Repels cabbage fly and ants.
- All mint varieties have similar properties.

Nasturtium

- Good to grow with many plants includin squashes, tomatoes, beans and some brassicas,

Oregano.

Nasturtium.

Rosemary.

- Avoid planting near cauliflower or radish.
- Said to be one of the best herbs for attracting predatory insects.
- Repels aphids, cucumber beetle and white fly.

Rosemary

- Particularly good to grow with beans, as well as carrots, cabbage and sage.
- Repels the bean beetle.
- Perfect companion herb for deterring many bean bugs.

Sage

- Similar to rosemary, good with beans, carrots and cabbage.
- Avoid growing basil near to sage. The basil probably won't thrive.
- Attracts honeybees.

Sage.

- Repels black flea beetle, carrot fly and cabbage fly.

PESTS AND DISEASES

As you can see from the companion planting list, herbs are probably one of the best deterrents of pests and diseases in the garden. They also attract the good bugs, which in turn dispose of many of the bad guys.

However there are a few bugs to watch out for, as follows.

Butterflies
Although beautiful, butterflies lay eggs on plants and the caterpillars that hatch will devour your plants with relish. Watch out for caterpillars on fennel in particular. If you spot butterflies landing on the plants, look on the underside of the leaves and rub the eggs off.

Aphids
Lots of foliage will attract aphids. If your plants are getting too many nutrients they may produce too much foliage too quickly and the plant will be weakened and vulnerable to aphid attacks. As long as the plants aren't fed regularly with fertilizers, they should stay relatively free from aphids. If you do get a problem, rub the aphids off with your fingers rather than using products to get rid of them.

Slugs and snails
These are the gardener's nightmare. They really can be tricky, and they are just as hungry as the hungriest caterpillar! Use any organic method of deterring them you can find. Coarse sand, grit or crushed eggshells spread around the plants are a good deterrent. These will wash away though, and you may have to repeat the process a few times until the plants are big enough to withstand a slug attack. Don't leave any spaces though. You may think it's only a tiny gap, but they will find a way!

Diseases

Diseases often follow after the plant has been weakened in some way, or there is a pollutant in the soil, but that is unlikely in a regular garden situation. Plants can become weakened by not having the right conditions in which to thrive.

Too much water
This could be the reason why many plants fail. In a very heavy soil, water logging may occur and the roots of your herbs will rot. Make sure the soil is well drained before planting and don't over-water.

Lack of water
This can also be an issue. Annual herbs and herbs with shallow root systems will need more water. The larger herbs with tap roots, or those herbs established over a few years will find water more easily, and will therefore tolerate drier conditions without too much harm coming to them.

Shade
If the plant doesn't get enough sunlight, photosynthesis doesn't occur and the plant won't thrive. There are a number of herbs that are happy to grow in shady areas, but most will need a certain amount of light, if not direct sunlight for a few hours every day.

Sun
On the other hand, some herbs don't like to be caught up in direct sunlight all the time and will shrivel and die very quickly. Many plants will benefit from a little protection from midday sun.

The simple needs of a plant can be taken care of

Although beautiful, butterflies lay eggs on plants and the caterpillars that hatch will devour your plants with relish.

with a little planning and so protecting your plants from becoming weak and vulnerable to disease.

Warm wet weather is the most creative and productive but also tends to attract more bugs and diseases. In extremely warm wet periods, some herbs can suffer from the following diseases:

Roots rotting – check the soil isn't too heavy for the herb.
Mildew – powdery bacteria which can affect basil.
Rust – mint will sometimes be affected by rust.

It is fairly rare for herbs to suffer from any of these diseases, but if they do, plants should be destroyed and new crops grown in a different area of the garden.

If your plants aren't growing as well as they should, run through the checklist above, considering water and sunlight conditions first. Your soil could be lacking in nutrients, in which case an organic feed might be useful. However, do this as a last resort as feeding herbs can weaken them and make them vulnerable to diseases and pests.

STORING HERBS

Wherever possible, herbs are best used fresh straight from the garden to the table. Some herbs die back in the winter though and can be dried or frozen to add a touch of summer to your winter meals.

Drying

There are a number of fairly easy methods to drying herbs. Sprigs can be hung up in a dark airy place until dry enough to crumble. This method is slightly more involved than it sounds. The stem of the herb will take longer to dry than the leaves and will need protecting from dust while hanging. Leaves can be dried separately on trays in the sun, in a home dryer or in a very slow oven. Leave the oven door ajar and keep the thermostat as low as possible. Drying too quickly can destroy the flavour.

When dry, leaves should be crumbled and stored in a sealed jar. Remember to label them if you are drying more than one herb.

Collecting seeds should be done with mature flower heads, hung upside down in paper bags until the seeds have fallen from the flower. Store seeds in a sealed jar for use in the kitchen or for planting next year. Again, remember to label.

Freezing

Many herbs will freeze successfully. Sprigs should be laid on a tray and frozen quickly. Place in freezer bags and label. Freezing changes the texture of most herbs, fruits and vegetables, and in some cases the flavour will be affected. If you can keep your herbs growing all year round always use them freshly picked.

CHAPTER 5

Twenty Everyday Garden Herbs

The following twenty everyday herbs can be grown in a moderate climate. Some can be grown indoors and most can be grown in containers:

- **Basil**
- **Bay**
- **Celery**
- **Chives**
- **Coriander**
- **Dill**
- **Fennel**
- **Garlic**
- **Horseradish**
- **Lavender**
- **Lemon balm**
- **Lovage**
- **Marigold**
- **Mint**
- **Nasturtium**
- **Oregano**
- **Parsley**
- **Rosemary**
- **Sage**
- **Thyme**

Herbs grown closely together can make an attractive display.

BASIL (*Ocimum basilicum*) (annual)

About basil

Basil is native to southern Asia and the Middle East but will grow as an annual plant in most moderate climates. It was introduced to Europe as a culinary herb in the sixteenth century.

Basil has, for many centuries, been considered to be a herb of love and purity and many myths and legends have been attached to it, from the belief that it will open the gates of heaven to that a sprig worn in the hair to attract your loved one.

It has been cultivated for thousands of years and has been used medicinally as well as in the kitchen for just as long.

Basil.

Basil can easily be grown in a pot.

Perhaps the most common use of basil today is its addition to tomato dishes and many people refer to it as the tomato herb. Basil was believed to cure many different ailments from coughs and colds through to digestive aids. It has also been used cosmetically to add shine to dull hair.

Properties

5 leaves of basil (2.5g)

Vitamin C	Calcium	Iron	Calories
0.5mg	4mg	0.08mg	1

Growing

Because basil is indigenous to warm regions, the plant will not survive cold temperatures. The seed should be started indoors in spring or outside when the ground has warmed up. Position basil plants with peppers and tomato plants and they will enhance each other's growth.

There are a number of different types of basil and you should choose one that is suited to your region. Most types of sweet basil will grow successfully in a moderate climate, if kept warm in the early stages of growth. It is possible to keep basil going throughout the winter but it will need to be indoors or in a warm greenhouse or conservatory.

If you want to try and keep plants going through the winter months, consider growing them in a container and then bring inside when the temperature starts to drop. Generally, plants should be watered less often during the winter months although in a centrally heated house, the soil may ry out quickly. Keep an eye on your plants and water when necessary.

Start your seeds off in trays, or pots of seed compost. Make sure the containers are well drained. Keep warm on a windowsill or in a greenhouse and keep the soil damp. Basil plants are normally fairly quick to germinate and you should see most of the plants up within the first couple of weeks of sowing.

When the plants have four or five true leaves (not counting the first two), they are ready to transplant. Pot on in individual pots or containers. When the weather and ground has warmed up, plant some straight out into the garden.

Choose a sunny spot. Basil likes lots of warmth and will thrive with five hours or more of sunshine every day. Prepare the soil by digging over and raking to a fine tilth. Remove any weeds and large stones.

Basil is not a heavy feeder and will tolerate a fairly poor soil. The plants stay fairly small and can be dotted about the garden. The heavy scent helps to repel flies and aphids so one or two plants in all your vegetable beds will help other crops resist bugs and viruses.

Because basil likes to grow in full sun, drying out can be a problem. Make sure you keep the plants well watered – but not waterlogged. The soil should always be well drained.

Seed can be planted directly outside, but the weather conditions must be good. Make sure all danger of frost has passed. Protect seeds and seedlings with a cloche at night if necessary. When the plants are a few inches high, they will need thinning and re-positioning if necessary. Basil repels insects so it doesn't tend to suffer with many problem bugs, although young plants should be protected against slug and snail attacks. Spread broken eggshells around the seedlings or use another organic method to put them off.

When the flower heads begin to grow, pinch out the whole branch and the plant will grow more leaves. Use your basil as much as you like. The more you use it, the more it will grow! Harvest the whole plant, or bring indoors in its container, before the cold weather. Frost or a very cold spell will finish off a basil plant.

Storing

Basil is always tastier if used fresh, but it can be stored very successfully by freezing or drying.

Hang sprigs or small bunches upside down in a dark, warm but airy room until dry. Crumble leaves into a sealable glass jar and label.

Freeze whole sprigs quickly on a flat tray and store in the freezer in sealable bags and label.

Medicinal uses for basil

Basil belongs to the same family of plants as mint and is considered to be a good digestive aid. Herbalists use it to help cure headaches, constipation and sickness. A small cup of basil tea after a meal aids digestion.

BAY (*Laurus nobilus*) (perennial)

About bay

Bay is native to Europe and some parts of Asia, and is an evergreen shrub. Bay trees will grow up to 15m (49ft) if they are left to their own devices and have enough space. For domestic gardens it is usually grown as a garden bush and kept to around 2m (6ft) in height.

A bay tree.

Bay leaves.

Its botanical name emphasises the respect once held for this plant. A rough translation is 'noble praise'. Bay leaves were strung into head-dresses and given to the victor as a crown, after physical combat.

Bay is known to have powerful antiseptic qualities, and it is one of the most ancient of all aromatic herbs. It is a woody plant and propagation is normally done by taking cuttings or layering. It does grow wild in some parts.

Bay is the chief ingredient in bouquet garni and no self-respecting chef would forget to add bay to soups and stews!

Properties

1 tsp crumbled bay leaf (0.6g)

Vitamin C	Calcium	Iron	Calories
0.3mg	5mg	0.26mg	2

Growing

Bay is usually grown from autumn cuttings or layering the branches. To take cuttings, simply prune the bush or tree back in the autumn and replant the cut stems. Use the pieces of stem with a 'heel' still on and strip all but three or four leaves. Dip the cut end in an organic hormonal product, if available, to speed up the root growth, although this isn't absolutely necessary. Plant by pushing the cut end into a fresh container, full of compost. Fairly large containers are very popular for growing bay. The tree is ornamental, evergreen and easy to maintain, and lends itself well to patio décor.

Once your cuttings are planted, stand back and let them grow. Water regularly and keep the container inside in a dark spot in the house. High humidity will give good results when propagating bay. A heated greenhouse is ideal, as long as the pot is kept in the dark. Place under a shelf and cover any low windows.

Don't use the leaves until the plant has developed roots and been re-potted or planted out.

Planting out your bay tree

A bay tree, once established and with a little maintenance, will survive for many years. Position the tree well. Give it lots of sun, keep it out of windy spots and well drained.

Dig a large hole for the roots to spread into, and mix some compost in with the soil you fill back in. Heel down firmly and water well. Keep weed free and watered during dry weather, and let it rest during the winter months.

Although an evergreen, the bay tree doesn't like the cold; in a cold winter climate it should be grown in a pot that can be brought indoors for a few months of the year.

Start using the leaves from your tree a few days after planting. Only pick what you need. Once established as a thriving outdoor herb, bay can be layered to produce more plants.

Layer propagation

Gently lay a branch down along the ground next to the plant without damaging either the branch or the mother plant. Using a u-shaped peg, secure the branch in the soil and cover with a fine layer of seed compost or other rich compost.

In about a year, roots should be sprouting and the new plant is safe to cut from the main plant. Re-plant in a pot or container or in another part of the garden. A young bay tree in a container makes a wonderful gift.

Seeds

Bay can also be grown from seed, although germination may be poor. The seeds take a long time to germinate and should be laid on top of moist compost in a container. Put a fine layer of dry compost over the seeds and keep in a dark place. Buy the seeds from a good garden centre, or a known seed company and you will get better results.

Check on the seed packet for the recommended time to sow seeds, according to your region, although generally seed should be sown in early to late spring.

Once you get the hang of growing bay from seed, there's no reason why you couldn't try collecting your own seed from the plants when they produce their fruits. The fruits aren't edible but the seeds are re-usable. Dry the seeds carefully and plant more than you would if you were using shop-bought seed.

General growing tips

Bay is a fairly hardy plant and is resistant to disease and pests, as many aromatic herbs are. Its worst enemy is the cold, and of course waterlogging. Always make sure your bush or tree has good drainage, and is protected or brought indoors during cold winters.

Keep weed free especially while the plant is young, and watered well enough to keep the soil moist but not wet. One of the main reasons potted bays die is lack of water. The leaves will start to go brown when the plant is lacking in water.

Prune to shape in the spring. If you leave the bay tree to grow without controlling it the tree will drain important nutrients from your garden, and become unruly. Container-grown bay trees should be pruned every year. Don't worry too much about the size of the pot. Bay doesn't mind being cramped, and will stay in the same container for about five years before it will need re-potting.

Storing

Bay is one of the easiest herbs to store – simply pick the leaves, brush them off and put them in a jar. They will start to lose their flavour after about twelve months. Unless you are cooking for many, only a few leaves are needed every few days or so, and therefore they can be used fresh.

Medicinal uses for bay

Bay isn't particularly known for its medicinal qualities, being more of a culinary herb, although it was once used externally as an antiseptic and to help relieve rheumatic pain.

CELERY (*Apium graveolens*)
(biennial – although some hybrids may be annual)

About celery

Although we consider it to be a vegetable, celery has been used as a herb for centuries. It was very important in Roman cuisine and also used medicinally. Celery was developed and cultivated into the vegetable we know today during the seventeenth

Celery.

century in Italy and later became popular in other parts of Europe.

Celery grows wild in many parts of Europe, Africa, south and north America, but it will not develop the blanched stalk unless cultivated. Grown as a vegetable in the kitchen garden, a few leaves can be picked and used in the kitchen for flavouring before the stalks have matured.

Wild celery, *apium graveolens*, is more resistant to pests and diseases than cultivated varieties.

Properties

1 medium stalk – 7 to 8in long (40g)

Vitamin C	Calcium	Iron	Calories
1.2mg	16mg	0.08mg	6

Growing

Celery will grow well in most moderate climates, but needs to be kept warm while germinating and until the plants are strong enough to be put outside.

Start your seeds by sowing in seed trays full of seed compost. Check on the growing recommendations on the seed packet for your particular region, but normally you would sow celery seed in early spring. Although the seed can take three or four weeks to germinate, they tend to be fairly prolific when they do start growing. The plants will be in the tray for quite some time and the seed should be sown fairly thinly. If you land up with hundreds of baby plants, you could thin them a little. Make sure the soil is very moist and then carefully pull out a few seedlings leaving space for the others to grow. Make sure you re-cover any exposed roots on the remaining plants.

The compost must be kept moist at all times so if you are starting them off in a warm conservatory or heated greenhouse, remember to water them regularly – a light spraying twice a day should be enough. The trays must also be well drained. Celery won't survive waterlogged soil.

When the plants get to about 10 to 15cm (4 to 6in) high, they should be planted out in rows in the garden. Wait until there is no danger of a frost before planting out, and the soil has warmed up a little.

Celery leaves.

One way to grow celery if you want to cultivate the stalks as well as the leafy tops, is to plant in trenches. Prepare the ground well, removing any perennial weeds and large stones, then add some compost to the soil. Make a trench and plant the celery leaving about 30cm (12in) between plants.

If you are growing for the foliage alone, the plant won't need earthing up later in the year, and planting in a trench isn't necessary. Leave about 15 to 20cm (6 to 8in) between each plant and plant in lines or in the herb garden.

Without the need for perfectly blanched celery stalks, the celery herb will grow happily in a well-drained container, as long as it gets regular water and is kept weed-free. Start using the leaves as soon as the plants are growing well.

To earth up celery plants, pull the earth gently from the surrounding area to cover the stalks. Use a light rake but be careful not to damage the plants. Some growers tie the celery stalks together to prevent them drooping and exposing the inner stalks.

Celery takes a long time to get going but the plants will last most of the year. Some varieties will carry on producing leaves into the following year before going to seed. Celery won't tolerate a frost so if you have your plants outside, bring them in as soon as the nights start getting colder. All blanched celery stalks must be harvested before the cold nights arrive.

Always double check on your seed packet for your regional growing recommendations. There are many different varieties of celery available and some will be more suitable to your needs than others.

Storing

Collect seed as it ripens in the autumn and use for flavouring. Leaves can be dried successfully and stored in a jar. As with most herbs though, the leaf is best used fresh. Celery leaf is stronger in taste than the stalk.

Medicinal uses for celery

Celery is used in ayurvedic medicine for bronchial problems, including asthma, wind and as a nerve tonic. Seeds collected when ripe are used to distil into oil and can be dried into powders. Seed sold for cultivation shouldn't be used medicinally.

CHIVES
(Alium schoenoprasum/sibiricum)
(perennial)

About chives

Chives are a member of the onion group, and grow wild in many parts of Europe and North America, although they originate from China. They have been collected from the wild for centuries but weren't cultivated until the middle ages. There are a number of different hybrids available including a garlic' (or Chinese) variety.

Chives are easy to grow and produce purple edible flowers that can be used to garnish a meal, or dried and used in a flower arrangement.

The bright green leaves are used in the kitchen and their delicate onion flavour enhances any meal.

Properties

tablespoon chopped leaves (3g)

Vitamin C	Calcium	Iron	Calories
1.7mg	3mg	0.05mg	1

Chives.

Growing

Chives are perhaps one of the easiest herbs to grow. They can be grown in pots outside or indoors on a windowsill. Placed in odd corners of the vegetable garden they will help deter pests from your crops, If you allow them to spread and they will take over a whole patch of your herb garden. Chive plants make an impressive border round a herb or vegetable plot. The one place you don't want to grow chives, however, is near to onions. The onion fly is one of the few bugs that attack chives.

They are a beautiful display plant, usually with purple flowers and always look fresh and green, as well as being edible.

From seed

Chives are one of the few plants in the onion family that are easy to grow from seed. Prepare a well-drained seed tray with seed compost and lightly sow the seed on the surface. Sprinkle a fine layer of compost over the seeds and water using a mister or fine spray. Keep the compost moist and the seed tray in a warm place.

Let the plants develop a little before planting out into pots or in the garden. It is a good idea to plant the small plants in pots for the first year and plant some out in the garden the following spring or summer. But as long as the baby plants are strong enough they can be planted directly outside in a warm, sunny spot. Plant out in the evening to allow them to settle in before the midday sun the next day.

Chives prefer a sunny spot but like a little shade when it gets very hot. The soil must be well drained and all you really need to do is water them occasionally. For outside planting, mix some potting

Chives can be grown in pots.

compost in with the soil you are planting into. If you are growing the plants on in pots or containers, use fresh potting compost and keep moist but not wet.

Root division

In the autumn, the plant can be divided, providing it's healthy and growing well. Gently fork up the whole plant taking care not to damage the roots, then carefully but firmly separate the clump of root into two or more pieces. Plant each piece out immediately and water in.

General growing tips

Choose a sunny position, although a little shade is preferable in high summer. The soil must be well drained. Chives will tolerate some drought, but will eventually need water. They won't need feeding unless your soil is particularly poor. If it is, then use an organic feed every few weeks.

Chives tend to stay fresh and green throughout the year but if your plants die back don't worry, the roots are probably fine and will produce fresh green leaves again in the following spring.

Harvest by cutting with scissors from the outside of the plant. Cut down to about 5cm (2in) in height. Herbs like to be used, so remember to cut them regularly. When the plant has finished flowering, cut the whole thing down to a couple of inches high and it will start producing fresh green chives again.

Storing

Chives stay leafy all year round so it is hardly worth storing them, but sometimes in cold weather they will die back. If yours are prone to do so, freeze a few bunches at the end of the summer. The flowers can be dried but the leaves won't dry successfully.

Medicinal uses for chives

Chives are primarily culinary herbs, but being part of the onion family, they do aid digestion, and they have also been used to help fight cold and flu symptoms. (However, onions are probably more effective.)

CORIANDER (*Coriandrum sativum* annual)

About coriander

Although we think of mint and parsley being the most common everyday herbs, coriander is perhaps the most widely used throughout the world. The fresh leaves are added to many dishes adding a unique spicy flavour, and the pungent seeds can be used in pickling or left whole in curries and spicy stews.

The seeds are also used in sweet dishes and coriander seed has been traditionally used in bread to aid digestion and improve the taste.

Coriander has been used for centuries as a flavouring herb. The Egyptians and ancient Greek physicians used it in many medical preparations. Chinese cultures believed it bestowed immortality and there have been findings of coriander seeds in tombs from over 5,000 years ago.

It is thought to be native to southern Europe and parts of Asia. The Romans spread the coriander word throughout Europe and it now grows wild in many regions.

Properties

sprigs (20g)

Vitamin C	Calcium	Iron	Calories
5.4mg	13mg	0.35mg	5

Growing

Coriander seed can take a little while to germinate. The seed should be sown in situ, as seedlings don't transplant well.

Prepare the ground by digging over and removing any perennial weeds and large stones. Rake to a fine tilth and sow the seeds in drills 4cm (1.6in) apart and about 1cm (0.4in) deep.

If you are growing coriander for the seed, you can encourage the plant to run to seed quickly by planting in a sunny position. The plants grown for foliage would appreciate a little shade during the hottest part of the day. When your plants start producing flowers, pick them off to encourage more leaf growth, or leave them to mature and produce seed.

Coriander.

Sow a short line every few weeks to keep a constant fresh supply, starting in early spring. If there is a frost expected, cover with a cloche overnight.

Coriander seed can also be sown by scattering them over a prepared bed and gently raking them over. Try this if you have plenty of seed to spare, so it won't matter too much if the birds get a few or the cat rolls in them.

Keep weed-free and watered well during very hot periods. When the plants are a couple of inches high they should be thinned to about 20cm (8in) of growing space per plant.

Coriander, like many herbs, thrives in containers or pots as long as they are well drained and kept watered. Keep a pot on the windowsill in the kitchen.

harvesting seeds rather than leaves, that won't be a problem, but if you are growing coriander specifically for the foliage, protect from full sun in the middle of the day. If your plants seem unhealthy, feed with an organic fertilizer every couple of weeks until they pick up. Avoid adding any other nutrients as this can affect the taste of the herb.

Storing

Coriander seed is used in kitchens all over the world. Wait until the seed is fully mature before storing. Lay a piece of card or cloth around the plant when you see the seeds starting to turn brown and then collect them as they fall.

The leaves can be dried and stored for many months before they lose their flavour. Hang stalks upside down in a dark, airy place indoors until dry. Crumble and keep in an airtight jar and label.

Medicinal uses for coriander

Although the ancient Chinese believed coriander bestowed immortality, it has yet to be proven. It does however aid digestion; you can chew the seeds as well as adding them to food. The bruised seeds are made into preparations for easing rheumatic pain.

Coriander can be grown in a pot.

Once established, a coriander bed can last for many years. Although an annual plant, it will re-seed itself if the temperature doesn't drop too low. Left to get on with it, a coriander patch can scatter itself to all parts of the garden, but it's not an invasive plant like mint. If it is in the way, pull it up and use it in the kitchen! Sow a short line of seed in the vegetable plot and look after it for the first year and it will keep coming back every year.

Coriander is strong smelling and deters aphids and other pests in the garden. The seeds are easy to collect. Keep some for cooking and some to plant the following spring. If you use your own seed for planting, sow a lot more than you would with a packet of hybrid seeds, as germination may be more erratic.

Coriander is fairly hardy and the only thing to watch out for is that it may bolt in the hot sun. For

DILL (*Anethum graveolens*)
(annual)

About dill

Dill has been around for centuries and was known to the ancient Greeks and Romans as a culinary and medicinal herb. The Romans saw dill as a sign of luck and the Greeks as a sign of wealth. It also has a long culinary history in India. The name is derived from the Norse word 'dilla' which means 'to lull'. Dill has been used extensively to soothe and calm.

In the Middle Ages it was considered to be an effective charm against witchcraft. The idea was that if you could encourage a witch to drink dill tea she would be too calm and soothed to be bothered with casting evil spells.

Dill has been a main ingredient in gripe water for

Dill.

...any years, and has been proved to soothe indiges-
...on, colic and general digestion problems.

The seed is produced extensively all over the
...orld. Dill pickle is probably one of the best-known
...ommercial foods using this herb.

Dill belongs to the same family as fennel and
...oks very similar, although the plants are smaller
...nd don't produce a large bulbous root.

Properties

sprigs (1g)

Vitamin C	Calcium	Iron	Calories
0.8mg	2mg	0.07mg	0

Growing

...ill is said to be one of the easiest herbs to grow
...ccessfully, so if you are just starting out in the
...arden, this is a good herb to start with. Dill doesn't
...eed to be started off indoors and should be sown
... situ. Dill plants grow quite tall and should there-
...re be positioned at the back of a herb or flower
...ed. However, they will like a sunny position and

one that is preferably sheltered from the wind as
much as possible.

Dill should not be planted near caraway or angelica. Although dill complements fennel, they can
sometimes cross-pollinate.

Prepare a seedbed outside in the spring and rake
to a fine tilth. Remove large stones and weeds, and
then sow your seed. Check on the seed packet for
manufacturer's growing recommendations for your
area, but you would normally plant the seed in mid
to late spring, after the coldest nights are over and
in time to get the early sun.

Make successive sowings every few weeks from
spring to summer so you will have a constant fresh
supply of leaves. In regions with mild winters, seed
can be sown right through until autumn.

Sow your seeds quite thickly so that the plants
support each other in the wind, or thin the plants
out to allow about 20cm (8in) of growing room
and support them with stakes. If you are using this
method, push the stakes into the ground before
planting so as not to disturb the roots later.

Caterpillars can be a problem for dill, so keep
an eye open and hand pick them off if necessary.
Chemicals should never be used on plants that are
to be eaten.

As with most herbs, dill can be grown in containers or pots and will thrive in a window box which
is carefully positioned and well-tended. The usual
conditions apply – well-drained and moist compost,

Dill plants.

but also care should be taken with wind. Dill grows tall and straggly and may need a stake or some form of support as it matures.

In the garden, plants growing close together help support each other, but one or two plants in a container or window box will need support.

Dill has long taproots, which find water more efficiently than other plants. In a container, however, it will need regular watering. Make sure the container or pot is fairly deep to allow the roots to take up nutrients from the soil properly.

Keep your plants free of weeds, and they should grow without too much interference. Outside plants need watering during extremely dry periods but otherwise can be left to find water on their own.

The best way to keep herbs thriving and producing leaf is to use them. Cut a few sprigs of dill regularly and the plant will push out more foliage.

Storing

Dill leaves are best eaten fresh but can be dried and stored in airtight jars for several months, although there will be some loss of flavour. The leaves can also be stored in a refrigerator for a few weeks. Collect the seeds and store in a jar for pickles and vinegar making. The flower heads and seeds are often used in making vinegars and oils.

Medicinal uses for dill

Dill has been used to aid digestive problems for many years – the best-known use is in gripe water for babies and young children. Make a tea out of an infusion of dill leaves or crushed seeds, and drink after a meal to help soothe stomach problems.

FENNEL (*Foeniculum vulgare*)
(biennial, perennial and sometimes cultivated as an annual)

About fennel

Fennel is indigenous to Mediterranean areas but has spread over many parts of the world. Fennel was one of the herbs held sacred by the Anglo-Saxons and it has been considered a powerful medicinal herb for centuries.

Fennel.

The ancient Chinese believed it would cur snakebites and the ancient Greeks believed it to b a helpful slimming aid. There seems to be a reviva of that opinion in recent years. Fennel certainl aids digestion and helps improve appetite.

In medieval times fennel was a herb used to repe witches, and has been used as an insect repellent It can cause other plants to run to seed or even di back entirely. Fennel works best in its own space.

The plants can grow to over 2m (7ft) tall and cover a large area. Fennel is a multi-purpose plant The seeds, leaves and bulbous root are all edible It is unlikely that wild or home-cultivated seed wil grow into a plant capable of producing a large bul bous root, but it will produce plenty of foliage. Bu hybrid seeds to cultivate the root.

Properties

100g of fennel bulb

Vitamin C	Calcium	Iron	Calories
12.0mg	49mg	0.73mg	31

fennel bulb.

Growing

Fennel is one of the easiest of herbs to grow if you are planning to use the leaves only. To produce a healthy swollen fennel bulb takes a little more practice. They only problem with fennel is that it tends to bolt (that is, run to seed) fairly quickly in the hot sun and sometimes when transplanted. Give it lots of water and keep it shaded from the midday sun for a week or two until it gets established.

Sow seed indoors in early spring. Use biodegradable pots, if possible, to reduce the risk of root damage when re-planting. Fill pots with fresh potting compost, and make sure whichever type of pots you use are well drained.

Keep warm and watered. Compost should be kept damp but not wet. When all danger of frost has passed, normally in late spring to early summer, plant out in the garden.

Choose a sunny spot at the back of a bed. The plants grow very tall and will shade lower-growing herbs or flowers. Fennel shouldn't be grown near tomatoes, beans, coriander or many other plants. It is best grown on its own or perhaps with dill.

Dig over the ground, fairly deeply if you are growing fennel for the root as well as the leaf. Remove any large stones and perennial weeds. Clean the ground of any non-organic debris and rake over until the soil is fine and ready for sowing. Make sure the soil is well drained and preferably on the light side. Fennel isn't fond of heavy clay soil. If you have heavy soil, a little sharp sand mixed into the soil first will help.

You can plant seed directly outside, as long as the nights are not too cold, and there is no possibility of frost. It is a good idea to cover seeds and young plants with a cloche overnight during the earlier months of the year.

Sow your seed according to the manufacturer's recommendations on the seed packet.

Fennel can be grown in pots and containers but should never be allowed to dry out.

When your young plants are coming up, keep watered and weed-free and watch out for caterpillars. Fennel is a great plant to grow where you may be having trouble with white fly in the garden as it repels it. But caterpillars are attracted to it, particularly the caterpillar of the swallowtail butterfly. While both the caterpillar and butterfly are very beautiful they will destroy your fennel plants. Keep an eye out for them.

Thin out the seedlings to about 30cm (12in) apart and rows about 60cm (24in) apart – the bulbs will start to swell later in the year. Make sure your plants get plenty of water during dry periods. Once the bulb is about the size of a tennis ball, they can be earthed up, but you should check the recommendations on your seed packet as there are many varieties of fennel available. After earthing up, cut down the foliage and allow the bulb to swell. The plant may sprout some new feathery leaves that are usable in late summer salads.

Fennel will tolerate several light frosts once mature and can be left in the ground well into the winter, especially if covered with a cloche or fleece. Dig up before very cold weather or prolonged frost.

Storing

The feathery leaves are best used fresh, but could be frozen or dried, if necessary. The seeds can be used before they are mature and can be stored for next years planting and adding to winter dishes and pickles. Pick the whole seed head and dry upside down in a paper bag to collect the seeds as they drop out.

Medicinal uses for fennel

Fennel is useful for aiding digestion and wind problems. It is used successfully as a mouthwash, to help treat sore throats and gum disease. It has also been proven to help in lactation.

GARLIC (*Allium sativum*)
(perennial or biennial, often cultivated as an annual)

About garlic

Garlic is part of the large group of plants belonging to the onion family and was cultivated as long ago as 3,000BC. Wild garlic has been around even longer. The Romans believed that garlic gave strength, and workmen and soldiers were encouraged to use it. It was also supposedly a good hangover cure in Roman times.

Garlic has been found in Egyptian tombs and was believed to be an offering to the gods. It was also used in embalming oils, and even now it is considered to be a useful preservative.

For centuries, garlic has been the number one herb for warding off vampires and bad spirits, and there are many myths and legends attached to it. Today we still use garlic in a number of medicinal preparations and it is widely believed to help protect against infections, including colds and flu. It is also used to treat many infectious diseases.

Properties

3 cloves (9g)

Vitamin C	Calcium	Iron	Calories
2.8mg	16mg	0.15mg	13

Young garlic plants.

Growing

Garlic is easy to grow and should be a part of every garden, not only for its wonderful culinary uses but because it will also help to deter pests and diseases from attacking your vegetable crops. Garlic is usually grown in lines, and is easier to cultivate and harvest if grown like this, but there is no reason why you couldn't scatter them in the garden. A few cloves here and there take up very little space.

Start off your crop by buying a bulb from your supermarket (choose an organic variety if possible) or buy bulbs specially cultivated for growing from your garden supplier.

Garlic can be planted early in the year. Prepare the ground as soon as it's workable. Choose a sunny, well-drained spot in the garden. Dig over and remove any large stones, perennial weeds and non-organic debris. Rake to a fairly fine tilth.

Place your separated cloves, flat root-end down in lines leaving about 20cm (8in) between each. Push them into the prepared soil and leave the top just slightly poking out of the ground. If you have trouble with birds however, push them in a little more or cover with a bird-friendly netting to protect the cloves until they start to shoot.

Keep the area watered but not too wet. Gener-
ly, garlic doesn't need too much watering early
the season. However, In a dry spring check the
round is fairly damp, and later in the summer,
ake sure the garlic is watered regularly.

Garlic doesn't suffer from pests or diseases. The
rong smell deters most bugs. And its anti-bacte-
al properties naturally protect it from infectious
iseases.

If your plants start running to seed, where they
ush up one strong stem and start flowering, bend
e stalk down to stop the flowering process. The
arlic bulbs from these plants should be used
arly as they are unlikely to store very well. Many
owers will simply pull up these rogue plants
d use them in the kitchen straight away. There
no harm in using cloves that are green, that is
efore they are left to dry, but they are stronger
sting.

By the end of the season each clove will be a
hole bulb. Depending on the weather through the
ummer months, the bulbs will mature any time
om July to September. When the plants start
ying back, protect them from too much rain to
void rotting.

Let the plants die back completely and then
ull up all the bulbs before the nights get too cold.
hoose a sunny day and loosen the soil around
ch plant carefully with a fork, then gently pull
em. Leave the whole plants out in the sun for a
ay then bring them in. Lay on racks or in boxes to
y before storing.

toring

arlic can be stored for many months. When the
aves are brown and dry, plait your bulbs and hang
em in a cool dark airy place. Keep a plait hanging
the kitchen. The cloves can also be dried indi-
dually, crushed and then kept in a glass jar to be
sed as garlic flavouring.

Medicinal uses for garlic

s well as being effective in preventing colds, flu
d infections, garlic is known to help reduce high
ood pressure, and high cholesterol. It has anti-
ngal and antibiotic qualities.

HORSERADISH (*Cochlearia armoracia*) (perennial)

About horseradish

Horseradish has been traced back to around
1,500BC. The ancient Greeks used it as a liniment
and it was also thought to have aphrodisiac powers.
Over the centuries horseradish has been described
as being worth its weight in gold and has been used
to cure everything from rheumatism to chest and
lung disease. It is believed to have originated in
central Europe and eventually spread to all parts of
Europe and north America.

As it became established as a herb that had ben-
eficial constituents, as well as being nourishing
and easy on the palate, horseradish became widely
used and commercialized. It is a prolific growing
plant and will become invasive in the garden if not
checked.

Horseradish root is commonly used as an accompaniment to fish and meat dishes – it is grated and
eaten raw. The young leaves are tasty and are suitable for adding to salads or in sandwiches.

Properties

1 tbsp (15g) prepared horseradish root

Vitamin C	Calcium	Iron	Calories
3.7mg	0.8mg	0.06mg	7

Growing

Horseradish is a prolific plant and should be
positioned carefully in the garden. To inhibit
rapid spreading, containers work well as they lit-
erally contain the plant. It will tolerate partial
shade but prefers a sunny spot if possible. Choose
a permanent place, as horseradish will last many
years.

Dig the ground deep and clear out any weeds,
large stones and non-organic debris. The cleaner
the soil, the bigger the roots will grow. More preparation will guarantee better crops. The horseradish
root likes a rich, well-manured soil and one that
is not too heavy. All root crops struggle in heavy
soils.

A horseradish plant.

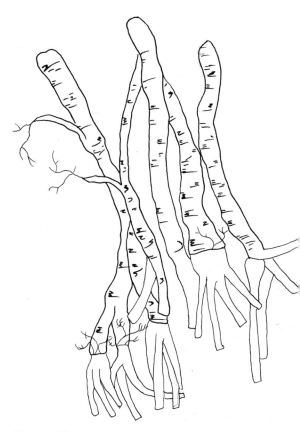

Horseradish roots.

If using containers, fill with organic compost and position in a sunny spot. Make sure the container is well drained, and kept watered and weed-free.

Horseradish is usually grown from root cuttings, which you can buy from reputable garden suppliers. Plant the root in early spring or autumn, but check with the supplier's growing recommendations, as the size of root, variety and regional concerns will vary. A neighbour or local gardener may be happy to donate a root or two to start you off. Plant as soon as possible after the roots have been lifted from the soil. Plant the roots according to how big they are. The smaller the root the shallower it should be planted.

Try taking your own root cuttings in autumn. Dig the roots up gently and use the largest one in the kitchen, then re-plant one or more of the side shoots.

Also, sections of root can be planted in the spring to produce new roots in autumn. Horseradish does spread quickly though and care should be taken not to let it take over the whole garden. For container growing, choose a large, well-drained container and fill it with fresh compost before planting.

From seed

Horseradish can be grown from seed sown in spring. The seeds should be sown in a sunny patch and the ground must be cleaned and dug deeply before sowing to allow for root growth. Again, the cleaner and richer the soil, the better chance you have of harvesting a good crop. Thin out the plants when they are a couple of inches high to allow space to grow. Keep weed-free and watered especially during dry periods.

Alternatively, sow seed in a large, well-drained container. Always use fresh compost when planting.

ut containers. Old compost will have been drained f some nutrients from previous plantings.

Once established, and with very little attention, he bed will become a permanent horseradish atch and will produce healthy roots for many ears.

Dig up all the roots every autumn. Use the larg- st roots in the kitchen and re-plant the others. his method of cultivation keeps your horseradish atch producing roots regularly and also helps to ontrol the rapid growth.

The young leaves can be used in salads and sand- iches. Take a few from each plant and allow them o grow again before using more. The root is cleaned, rated and eaten raw, often mixed with vinegar and ream and served with a Sunday roast.

Horseradish root is said to be stronger tasting fter the first frost, so if you can leave them in until hen, you will get a better result.

toring

tore cleaned roots in a paper bag for up to a eek in the fridge. After that the taste will dimin- h and they will start to shrivel. Smaller roots can e stored in sand for planting out in the spring. he best way to store horseradish is to make a auce and seal in airtight glass jars. Leaves should e used fresh.

Medicinal uses for horseradish

Horseradish root can be made into a syrup to ease ronchitis, coughs and colds. The sliced raw root also said to be effective in treating boils, and fected wounds. Large doses can cause sickness, nd horseradish remedies aren't advisable for peo- le with stomach ulcers or thyroid problems.

ENGLISH LAVENDER
(*Lavandula angustifolia*)
(perennial)

About lavender

Lavender is probably one of the most well-known erbs and is grown practically all over the world. or centuries it was used as a medicinal herb and

historically was used to flavour food to help calm the stomach.

Lavender has antiseptic qualities, and has been used in medicines and ointments as early as Roman times. The ancient Egyptians used it in embalming fluids and also placed it in the tombs of royalty. The ancient Greeks would have used it to treat insect bites, stomach disorders and kidney problems.

Lavender water was believed to cure fainting, nausea and dizziness for many generations. It's also a favourite ingredient in detergents, air fresheners and pot-pourri mixtures used at home and work. Lavender clears the head and freshens the environ- ment.

Lavender flowers produce an oil which is employed in many preparations – perfumes and similar products. The flowers are also useful nectar- producing plants, which in turn yield high-quality honey.

Properties

Lavender is used to provide the volatile oil, found in the buds or flowers of the plant. In dried flow- ers, up to 3% of oil can be extracted, and in fresh flowers up to 0.5%. The chief constituents of the oil are linalool and linalyl acetate. Lavender oil is soluble in alcohol.

Growing

Lavender grows as a small shrub ranging from about 15 to 60cm (6 to 24in) tall and prefers a sunny and dry position. Choose your spot well and lavender will continue to be part of the herb garden for many years. Lavender plants can live for up to thirty years in the right environment. Make sure the ground is well drained. Lavender grows well in raised beds and resting on stone walls.

Lavender is happy to grow in most soils but the optimum conditions would be in a dry, sandy soil and one which is not too acidic. Add a little lime before planting if you have acid soil. Dig the ground well in the autumn before planting and remove any weeds and non-organic debris.

The best method of starting lavender plants is from cuttings. Take cuttings of young branches

Lavender.

from a well-established plant, in late summer to early autumn. Make sure the branches have a 'heel' and plant in a warm environment until the following spring when they can be transplanted out in the garden. Transplant in lines allowing space to grow, or simply plant one or two in a decorative area of the garden. A well-drained sunny spot anywhere in the garden will do.

Lavender can also be planted from seed, but germination can be a bit erratic. Start the seed in well-drained pots of fresh compost and keep in a warm greenhouse or other bright, warm place. Keep the soil clear of weeds and watered sparsely but kept slightly moist until germination.

When the seedlings are strong enough to handle, transplant them to the garden. Water sparsely, never allowing the plant to become too wet or the roots too waterlogged. When the plants start producing flowers in the first year of growth, cut

Lavender flowers.

em down to encourage growth in the main
lant. The more foliage and new branches it pro-
uces in the first year, the stronger the plant will
ecome.

English lavender is the hardiest variety available
nd will tolerate very cold winters. If the ground
; not too wet, though, just before winter mulch
) protect the roots from extreme cold. Remove
ulch early in spring.

From the second year let the flowers grow; laven-
er is a hardy plant and appreciates being used, so
on't restrict yourself from cutting the stalks when
equired. A few dried sprigs of lavender keeps the
lothes' drawers and wardrobes smelling fresh. If
ou are feeling industrious, sew a tiny cushion with
ried lavender flowers inside. This can be popped
1 a drawer or under a pillow to ensure a good
ight's sleep. Lavender plants are aromatic and
race any garden left to their own devices. How-
ver, it is a good idea to use the herb to encourage
1ore growth and to benefit from their wonderful
roperties.

If the shrubs are getting straggly, trim them to
1ape in autumn and protect them from severe
old. The English lavender variety will tolerate
ery low temperatures, but as mentioned before
1ulch can help it rest well during the winter
1onths.

toring

Lavender rarely needs storing, but the flowers
re only available until late summer or autumn,
epending on the variety. Pick flowers and dry
1em in the sun or a home dryer. Don't dry too
uickly. The flowers can be stored in a glass jar.
Jse in recipes, pot-pourri mixtures and as drawer
esheners. Lavender-based products make mar-
ellous gifts.

Medicinal uses for lavender

The medicinal uses for lavender would require
nother book to list them all. A sachet filled with
ried lavender flowers and placed under the pil-
ow will ensure a good night's sleep. Lavender
ea is helpful in alleviating stress headaches and
1igraines, as well as indigestion and colic.

LEMON BALM (*Melissa officinalis*)
(perennial)

About lemon balm

Lemon balm is a shrub normally growing up to
around 60cm (2ft) high. It is perennial but the
foliage dies back during the winter months. It can
be slightly invasive but can be grown in containers or cut back to control its growth. The bruised
leaves release a fresh lemon smell, which makes it
an excellent plant to grow next to pathways or seating areas.

Lemon balm originated in the Middle East but
is now widely grown throughout the world. It was
once thought to cure all ailments and has long been
used to relax the body and soothe the nerves.

Lemon balm.

A popular preparation with lemon balm as the main ingredient was used throughout the seventeenth century and was known as Carmelite water. It was invented by Carmelite monks and nuns in the early part of the century in Paris, and was used as an eau de cologne and a cordial. Lemon balm leaves were infused with zest of lemon, coriander, nutmeg and root of angelica. Carmelite water was also taken to alleviate pain from neuralgia and nervous headaches.

Properties

Lemon balm is a good source of tannin, which aids digestion and is anti-bacterial and anti-fungal. *Rosmaric* acid is also present and is a potent antioxidant being many times more powerful than vitamin E or C. The essential oil contains citral and citronella.

Growing

Lemon balm is attractive to bees and in turn produces good-quality honey. It is often found growing wild in light woodland areas, and in parkland where there is some shade.

The plants should be placed in a sunny part of the garden that also gets some shade, and somewhere fairly permanent. The leaves will die back during the winter but the roots stay alive in the ground and will shoot again in the spring. In a very dry climate lemon balm will be better in partial shade. In very cold winters it may be wise to protect the plant by placing a garden fleece or cloche over it during the coldest months.

Lemon balm is drought tolerant once established and shouldn't need watering too often. It likes a light well-drained soil. If the plant has ideal growing conditions, it will re-seed itself and continue to get bigger as the years go by. It can be invasive, but parts of the root can be dug out to make room for other plants. Done carefully, this will not affect the main plant.

Dig over the ground and mix in some rich, well-rotted manure or compost. Remove any weeds, large stones and non-organic debris.

Lemon balm leaves.

Cuttings

Lemon balm propagates well from cuttings. Take young cuttings in the autumn from an established plant and set out in the ground approximately 30cm (12in) apart, leaving enough space for each plant to grow, The cuttings can be started in a container either as a permanent or temporary home. Not all cuttings will take, so it is a good idea to plant as many as you have space for. By the following spring the cuttings will have produced roots – discard the ones that haven't. In July or August plant out the cuttings that have roots and are growing well into their permanent positions.

Propagation can also be done by root division during spring or autumn. Dig up the plant very carefully to avoid damaging the roots. Separate into clumps and re-plant into containers or a seedbed until they become established and can be planted out into their permanent positions the following year.

From seed

Lemon balm can be started from seed, but germination can take some time and the seeds must be protected from birds, other wildlife and weather conditions until they germinate.

Sow the seed in well-drained seed trays of compost and keep in a cold frame. The seed can be sown in spring or autumn. As soon as the plants are large enough to handle, pot up and look after them until they are at least 15cm (6in) in height, when they can be planted out in the garden or a permanent container.

While getting established, lemon balm will need damp, but not wet, soil. The plant won't cope with waterlogging and, if grown in containers, it is very important that the containers are well drained.

Use leaves as often as required and harvest sprigs for storing just before or just after the plant has flowered.

Storing

Lemon balm leaves keep their scent well, and can be dried and stored successfully for many months in a glass jar. The plant produces lush foliage for a large part of the year and only needs to be stored for the winter months. The leaves are useful for lemon teas and for pot-pourri mixes.

Medicinal uses for lemon balm

Lemon balm is another herb that has multi-medicinal qualities. A lemon tea can soothe the nerves and, mixed with a little zest of lemon and a spoonful of honey, will help alleviate the symptoms of colds and flu. Fresh leaves are better than dried for making tea. The leaves are soothing after insect bites and will deter mosquitoes if you rub the leaves onto your skin. A lemon tea at night is said to be relaxing and sleep inducing.

LOVAGE (*Levisticum officinalis*) (perennial)

About lovage

Lovage is a hardy perennial plant and will last for many years given the right growing conditions. It will also grow anything from 0.9m to 2.2m (3ft to 7ft) tall, so needs to be placed at the back of a bed so as not to overshadow lower growing plants.

Lovage has a strong taste, familiar to celery, and is often used as a substitute for celery salt. The seeds are ground to make salt, and the leaves are used for flavouring stews and soups. The leaves can also be added to the salad bowl. Some cultures strip the bark off the plant and eat the stem raw as a vegetable, although generally the plant is used for its foliage and seed. Lovage is high in vitamin C content.

Originally from Mediterranean areas, lovage has adapted well to cooler climates. It grows well in the United Kingdom and other parts of Europe.

Lovage has been used for many centuries in culinary and medicinal preparations.

Properties

Lovage is known to be a good source of vitamin C, although the essential oil is the magic ingredient

Lovage.

Lovage leaves.

responsible for the taste, smell and medicinal properties. The flowers and seeds produce the most oil, but all parts of the plant, leaves, stem, root, flowers and seeds are rich in essential oils.

Growing

Lovage is a hardy perennial and will survive fairly harsh winters. The foliage may die back but will return in the spring. It likes a sunny spot, although will tolerate partial shade. The plants should be positioned at the back of a bed. It's not a suitable herb to grow indoors or in containers as it grows very tall, although it can be grown against a fence or wall as long as it has enough sun.

The ground should be well drained, and dug over well. Lovage likes a deep rich soil and well-rotted manure or compost should be dug in during the spring if you are planting the following autumn, or in the autumn if you are planting in the following spring.

From seed

Remove all weeds and large stones and rake to a fine tilth before sowing seed in the spring. Sow the seed, but check first with the supplier's growing recommendations, as there are a few different varieties. When the seeds have germinated plant out the baby plants as soon as they are big enough to handle in their permanent position. Allow about 60cm (2ft) between plants. If you have too many young plants try placing them in quiet corners around the garden or pot them up and give them away as gifts.

The seeds can also be started in well-drained seed trays full of rich seed or potting compost, and planted out later.

Keep your plants weed-free and watered until they become well established.

Root division can also start off lovage. Dig up a healthy plant, carefully digging around the roots to avoid damage. This should be done in spring, just after the leaves start to show. The roots can be gently pulled apart and divided into two or more sections. Re-plant the pieces that have a growing shoot, in well-prepared ground, about 60cm (2ft) apart. Water, and keep the ground fairly moist while the plants get re-established.

Create more foliage by picking off the flowers as they appear. Or if you want the seed, allow it to fully ripen and then store or re-plant. The seeds are best sown when they are just ripe which means an autumn sowing. In cooler climates the young plants may need to be protected with a cloche or similar cover until the spring. You can keep the seed to plant in the spring; they will need to be kept in an airtight container and out of direct light.

Lovage will die back in the winter leaving a few collapsed stems, which can be cut down. However ladybirds like to hibernate in these stems so leave them to die back naturally if you can.

Lovage grows well and will last a few years before the plant gets tired. At that point, root division can be a good way to re-start your plants.

Storing

The seeds of lovage can be stored for many months and can be used for re-planting the following year or in cooking. The seeds can be ground and used as a 'celery' salt. The leaves can also be dried and kept in a sealed jar to add to stews and soups through the winter.

Medicinal uses for lovage

Lovage has been used in many medicinal preparations for centuries and has been considered to be something of a wonder drug. It is known to stimulate the appetite, and help cure indigestion. It was also added to baths at one time to deodorize and cleanse the skin.

MARIGOLD (*Calendula officinalis*) (annual)

About marigold

The *Calendula officinalis* plant is the original old-fashioned pot marigold and has been traditionally grown in herb gardens all over Europe for centuries. Native to southern Europe, the marigold has spread, and now grows wild in the United Kingdom.

Marigold was also used in early Indian and Greek cultures as a flavouring and colouring for food. It was believed to have magical qualities and was often used to decorate whole villages in times of celebration.

Marigolds are not only one of the best-known herbs, they are also one of the most useful. The plant yields a yellow dye as well as being an effective medicinal and culinary herb.

It is also a useful companion herb. Marigolds deter pests very effectively and are often planted all over the garden; in amongst the vegetables and fruit crops, as well as in the herb garden. They have bright yellow or orange blooms and will flower throughout the growing season. They are a must-have in the garden.

Properties

Marigold is known to have many healing properties which include volatile oil; *calendulin* and *saponins*, all of which aid in healing and digestion. The leaves are thought to be high in vitamin C but there is little data available. Primarily calendula is grown for flavouring and medicinal purposes.

Marigolds.

A marigold flower.

Growing

The true marigold (*Calendula officinalis*) is stronger tasting and has more medicinal qualities than the French and African hybrids (*Tagetes*). Although these hybrids are worth growing, your true herb garden should include the *Calendula*.

Marigolds are a magic plant to have in the garden – spread them everywhere. They look sunny and bright and they also deter many pests, which keeps other crops bug-free. Not only do they look pretty in the garden, but they also attract ladybirds, which is even better. No garden should be without them.

The one pest that will get your marigold crop is the slug. Do anything you can to avoid the slug problem. Hire in some toads, or use a traditional method of deterring them. Broken eggshells laid around the plant helps, but is a bit laborious. Or try a dish of beer – it attracts the slugs and they fall in and drown. You may have a lot of drunken slugs to deal with in the morning though!

Marigolds like a sunny spot but will be able to tolerate partial shade. You can sow seed directly into the ground outside in late spring. But they will need thinning and spacing, so it's usually best to grow them in containers earlier in the year.

Sow the seed thinly in seed trays of compost and water once. Make sure the trays are well drained and keep in a sunny spot indoors or in a warm greenhouse until the plants have germinated and grown large enough to handle. Marigolds germinate easily and shouldn't need to be watered again before they shoot, but keep an eye on the soil drying out if kept on a sunny windowsill.

When the seeds have germinated they will need a little water to keep them growing well. When the plants are large enough to handle, they can be transplanted into the garden.

Transplant your marigolds in sunny or semi-shaded areas of the garden. Scatter them around to help protect other crops and to bring a splash of colour all over the garden. Plant carefully and allow about 15cm (6in) between plants if planting together. Plant two or three in one spot if you have enough plants.

Marigolds do very well in containers and in pots indoors. Water your plants a couple of times a week, perhaps more if they are growing in containers or in very sunny dry spots. Mulching helps to control weed problems.

Remove flower heads as they die back to encourage more blooms. A few flowers can be left to mature into seed development. The seeds can then be collected when ripe.

Marigolds will start flowering in mid-summer and will carry on right through until the first frost. This is not a frost-hardy herb.

Storing

Marigold flowers can be dried and stored in sealed jars for some months. Make sure the flower is totally dry before storing. Dry by hanging, or on a tray in a very cool oven for a few hours. Use a home dryer if you have one. Marigold flowers make a soothing tea.

Medicinal uses for marigold

The medicinal uses for marigold are too numerous to mention. Marigold has been proved to have wonderful healing properties. These are a few everyday remedies worth knowing about:

- If rubbed on the affected part, a marigold flower will soothe the pain and swelling of a bee or wasp sting.
- An infusion made from the leaves eases sore feet.
- Creams and lotions that are calendula-based are highly effective in treating minor burns, wounds, inflamed areas of skin, and insect bites.

MINT (PEPPERMINT) (*Mentha piperita*) (SPEARMINT) (*Mentha spicata*) (perennial)

About mint

Mint is probably one of the best-known herbs in the United Kingdom, if only for its accompaniment to roast lamb! The essential oil in mint is used in many medicinal and cosmetic preparations as well as in the kitchen.

It is a hardy perennial and a prolific grower. It is suitable to grow in pots and containers as well as directly in the herb or vegetable garden, in shady spots where nothing else seems to grow. It is prolific though and will take over a large area rapidly if not contained. Mint will often come back a couple of years after it has been removed from the area. Plant it where it won't disturb the rest of the garden.

There are about 1,000 different types of mint but only about five or six of these are worth cultivating. Peppermint is the most popular and probably the most useful variety. It can be used in sweet and savoury dishes and is a recognized healing herb. Spearmint and pennyroyal mint are also popular varieties to grow at home. There will usually be a choice of varieties available in your garden centre.

Mint has been used as far back as Roman times and has been cultivated in Europe for many years, although there wasn't a lot recorded about the plant until the seventeenth century.

Properties

tbsps mint (3.2g)

Vitamin C	Calcium	Iron	Calories
1.0mg	0.8mg	0.16mg	2

Mint.

Growing

Mint will grow in virtually any spot and will take over the whole area if not checked. It is very suitable for container growing but also will do well in a shady part of the garden, where perhaps not much else will grow.

Ideally mint should be contained. Plant in a container that has been sunk into the ground, or alternatively in pots on the windowsill or outside on the patio.

Dark mint.

Like most herbs, mint prefers a rich, well-drained soil but likes moisture so a shady spot is ideal where the soil doesn't dry out too quickly. The area mustn't be waterlogged though. Dig over the ground and mix in some well-rotted manure or compost during the season before planting.

It's very important to contain mint unless you want a field of it. Sink a bottomless container such as an old bucket with its base cut out into the ground, or dig a deep hole and line with black plastic. This won't contain the plant one hundred percent, but it will help. Alternatively, stick to container growing.

Mint will propagate easily from seed as well as by separating the roots and re-planting. Sow seed in early spring and keep moist and weed-free until the plants are large enough to handle. Then pot them up or plant in the garden.

To propagate by root division, simply break off the root and re-plant in potting compost until it has established a good root system and then plant it out.

Garden centres and plant suppliers often have pots of mint ready to plant out. Look at the labels before buying – there are many different varieties available including eau-de-cologne mint, which isn't very suitable for mint sauce, but will produce a lovely scent in the home if grown indoors.

Mint is a hardy plant and doesn't need an awful lot of looking after but an occasional mulch will help keep the moisture in the roots. The roots are shallow and can dry out too much if left. This should only need doing if the plant is growing in full sun or there hasn't been much rainfall.

Mint can occasionally suffer with a rust disease and should be removed and burnt. Plant new plants away from the affected area. This disease can be caused by bad drainage, too much water generally or simply a virus in the soil.

Pick leaves as you need them, and remove the flowers to produce more foliage.

Storing

Hang sprigs upside down in a dust-free area, or hang in paper bags. The leaves can then be crumbled and stored in an airtight jar to be used for flavourings and mint tea. Mixing fresh leaves with vinegar is another way to store mint (add sugar to make mint sauce, which is often served with lamb). Again, keep in sealed jars.

Medicinal uses for mint

Mint is well known for its medicinal qualities, and is regularly drunk as a tea or eaten in the form of a candy after meals to aid digestion. Many people swear by a cup of mint tea every day to keep cold and flu away. It is also a good remedy for nervous headaches and stress.

NASTURTIUM (*Tropaeolum majus*)
(perennial, in colder climates an annual)

About nasturtiums

Nasturtiums are a trailing vine plant and can be used for excellent ground cover or trained to climb a trellis or fence. There are various hybrids on the market that will be suitable for either ground cover or climbing. They have been likened to watercress in the past. The leaves of both plants have a peppery taste and are high in vitamin C content.

Nasturtium flowers have been used to decorate homes as well as food for centuries and are an excellent addition to a salad bowl. The leaves are also used in salads and add a peppery taste to the meal.

The seeds can be used instead of more expensive capers, and are a good pickling spice. Nasturtiums will re-seed if the conditions are right and you may find them coming up all over the garden. They are a wonderful addition to the herb garden.

Properties

Although known to be high in vitamin C content, there is little data about the other components of nasturtiums. It is said to have similar qualities to watercress, but that could be because the leaves have a very similar peppery taste.

Growing

There are a number of different nasturtiums available, but to be sure of a good-tasting and decorative herb, use the *Tropaeolum majus* variety. This is a hardy variety and will probably re-seed itself year after year given the right conditions.

Nasturtiums are probably one of the easiest herbs to grow. Buy ready-grown plants from a nursery or garden centre and set them about 30cm (12in) apart in the ground, or slightly closer together if you grow them in containers.

Or start them off with seed. In some areas, you may only ever need to buy one packet of seeds.

Nasturtiums.

The plants will re-seed and come up year after year. Choose a sunny and well-drained spot. Dig over your soil well, and remove any perennial weeds and large stones. Don't dig in any compost or manure. If the soil is too rich you will get more leaves than flowers.

Plant your seeds about 20 to 30cm (8 to 12in) apart and water. Keep the weeds away and water well. Nasturtiums should be kept watered during the whole growing season. When the flowers start arriving, you can ease off a bit, but they should never be allowed to dry out. Although they need a lot of water, the ground should still be well drained and definitely not waterlogged.

They grow well in containers and should be planted about 20cm (8in) apart or slightly less. Make sure the container is well drained and kept in a sunny spot, but don't allow the soil to dry out.

Nasturtiums will also grow successfully climbing a trellis or similar structure. Guide the vines as they grow and secure to the structure, using loose ties.

Pick the leaves and flowers as you need them. The plants will keep producing flowers for many months and the leaves will be available even longer.

Nasturtiums grow well around cucumbers and are a good companion plant. Also, because of their ground coverage and damp soil, they provide good cover for frogs and toads that in turn get rid of a fair number of slugs. So to keep slugs off your cucumbers, and other squashes, grow nasturtiums with them.

Because of the dense, low foliage, nasturtiums will also help blanch a crop of leeks if grown around them.

At the end of the season this versatile plant produces seed which can be left on the plant to drop and re-seed itself next year. The seed can be collected when ripe and used in the kitchen.

Storing

When fully ripe, the seed should be stored in sealed glass jars for using as pickling spice or flavourings in the kitchen. Store some seed to plant in the spring in case they don't come up on their own. The leaves and plants have a high water content and don't store well, although leaves will stay fresh in a fridge for a couple of days.

A nasturtium flower.

Medicinal uses for Nasturtiums

Nasturtium seed has an anti-bacterial property which can aid in treating minor skin eruptions and respiratory problems. It has a high vitamin C content, which is also useful for treating minor skin conditions.

OREGANO (*Origanum vulgare*) (perennial)

About oregano

Oregano is also known as wild marjoram. Both herbs belong to the *Origanum* family, but they are different. Oregano originated in the mountains of Greece and was thought to produce a more flavoursome meat from the goats that grazed on it. It spread across the Mediterranean area, and now grows freely in many parts of the world, especially in Southern Italy, and is a viable commercial product in Europe and Mexico.

Oregano grows as a low bush and in mild cli

Oregano.

nates will stay green throughout the year. As with ny leafy herb, the strength of flavour and aroma depend greatly on the temperature and water upply.

It was considered to be of high medicinal value n Roman times, and for centuries has been used n medicinal preparations. Oregano is packed with ninerals and vitamins and plays a strong role in ealing minor ailments.

Properties

This table shows just a few of the many minerals nd vitamins oregano contains.

1 tsp of dried oregano leaf (1g)

Vitamin C	Calcium	Iron	Calories
0.5mg	16mg	0.44mg	3

Growing

Oregano plants last three or four years before they need replacing. The seeds tend to germinate well. One way of sowing seed is by sprinkling onto pots of warm compost and spraying with water on a daily basis, probably two or three times a day. You can start the seeds off like this quite early in the year as long as they are kept warm. Keep the pots

Oregano leaves.

in a warm greenhouse or on a windowsill, but make sure they don't get too much sun before germinating. Keep the soil moist.

When the plants are large enough to handle, thin out to allow enough space for them to grow. If you are keeping them in the pots, pull out the weaker one and leave only one plant per pot. (Sow two or three seeds per pot if you intend to do this).

Oregano is well suited to container growing, and will grace a patio, brighten up a kitchen windowsill or look stunning in a hanging basket. It will also enhance a herb or vegetable garden.

Oregano has startling bright leaves and provides a pretty ground cover as well as deterring pests from a veggie patch. Grow a few plants around sweet peppers to provide the humid atmosphere peppers thrive on.

In late spring, or after all danger of a frost has passed, oregano seed can be sown directly outside. Plant in a well-drained seedbed and keep watered and weed-free. Thin the young plants out when they are large enough to handle to give them enough space to grow. A well-established oregano plant may spread to a few feet across, but they can be trimmed back if too unruly.

It is a good idea to check on the recommended growing instructions on your seed packet if you have one, as varieties differ. Times of planting are affected by your region's climate, and some hybrid varieties will need more space than others.

As soon as the seeds have germinated reduce watering. Oregano should never be watered in damp conditions.

The foliage dies back in the winter but will return the following spring. In very cold winters it's advisable to protect your plants with mulch. Although, if you do have severe winters, you may consider growing herbs in containers that can be brought inside during the cold months. Oregano is a suitable container herb. The container doesn't have to be very large, but must be well drained. Put a layer of gravel in the bottom of the container before filling with compost. Oregano needs very good drainage to thrive.

The plant can be trimmed back and shaped, although this can be done as you use it. Use oregano often and it will produce more leaves. Pick the flowers off as they appear, to produce more foliage. If you want the plant to flower, harvest plenty of leaves before the flowers start to appear.

Pick just a few leaves until the whole plant is about 20cm (8in) high then cut as much as you want and it will keep growing back.

Oregano is a wonderful herb for deterring aphids, including green and black fly. Position your oregano plants in sunny spots around the garden to help keep aphids away. Because of their spectacular foliage oregano plants provide spectacular focal points.

Storing

Oregano can be dried by hanging upside down in brown paper bag and then crumbled and stored in sealed glass jars. The herb is available fresh for much of the year though and, as with most herbs the taste does deteriorate with drying.

Medicinal uses for oregano

Oregano is used in preparations to soothe sore throats and coughs in children. It has been used in digestive cures as well as many other general disorders, including influenza. Oregano is also a highly effective antiseptic and has sedative qualities. Large doses should not be taken.

PARSLEY (*Petroselinum crispum*)
(biennial)

About parsley

Parsley has traditionally been used as a food garnish and flavouring, for head-dresses and even for adorning tombs during ancient Greek times.

It is probably the most under-used herb in the garden but is rich in vitamins and minerals, particularly iron. Gram for gram, parsley has more vitamin C than most citrus fruits.

There are a number of different varieties. The most commonly used are the curly leaf and Italian flat leaf types which are added to many recipes, as well as being an attractive garnish.

Parsley originally grew wild in Mediterranean areas, but has been cultivated throughout Europe and America for many centuries.

In recent years, the remarkable properties of parsley have been well documented and the herb is freely used in professional and home kitchens, although there is still a temptation to use it only as a garnish.

Parsley is effective for freshening the breath after eating garlic.

Properties

10 sprigs of parsley (10g)

Vitamin C	Calcium	Iron	Calories
13.3mg	14mg	0.62mg	4

Growing

Parsley likes to grow in a sunny spot, and thrives in a rich soil. It grows well in containers and can be dotted around the garden to grow with other herbs and vegetables. Varieties of parsley differ so much that sometimes it is hard to tell they come from the same family. Try growing flat-leaved and tight, curly-leaved varieties to compare.

Parsley.

Buy ready-grown young plants from a nursery or garden centre to get your crop going quickly. But these plants are often started in forced conditions and are not hardened to cold nights. It's unlikely the plants would survive if put out too early. Keep plants well watered, on a sunny windowsill – this way a healthy parsley plant will keep green and fresh right into the winter months. They may be transplanted a little later in the year.

Always ensure pots are well drained, but remember that parsley needs to be kept moist, so water pots regularly.

Choose a well-drained sunny spot outside. Parsley will tolerate some shade but the soil will need to be rich in nutrients for it to thrive. Dig over the ground and remove any perennial weeds and, if available, dig in some well-rotted manure or rich compost.

From seed

Parsley will grow readily from seed, but can take more than six weeks to germinate, so it needs to be started in clean compost where the seeds won't be drowned with weeds. Some growers soak the seed for twenty-four hours before planting, to speed up the germination process.

Sow a few seeds in pots, and keep warm and the soil moist. When the plants come up, thin to one plant per pot. The seedlings you remove could be planted elsewhere, but consider how many parsley plants you may need. The thinning-outs may be better off in the salad bowl.

Seeds can be planted directly outside, but not until the weather is warmer. As parsley needs a long growing period, it is generally better to start them in early spring in a greenhouse, or indoors.

When all danger of a frost has passed, young plants can be transplanted into the garden and containers can be put outside. Parsley is a heavy feeder, resulting in iron and mineral rich leaves. If your soil could be lacking in nutrients, parsley will benefit from a regular organic feed.

Start using the leaves when the plants are at least 20cm (8in) tall and use them throughout the year. During the second year of growth, parsley will produce flower and seed. The seeds can be collected when ripe.

Parsley has a long taproot and tends to look after

Parsley can be grown in pots.

itself fairly well once it settles in, but it should never be allowed to dry out. Water regularly.

Storing

For seed collection: hang flower heads upside down in a paper bag when the seed has started to form. Leave in a dry, airy place until the seeds drop from the rest of the plant, then store seed in a sealed jar.

Parsley leaf can be dried: hang the whole stems or lay on racks to dry, then crumble leaves and store in sealed jars and label. Whole stems of parsley can also be frozen.

Medicinal uses for parsley

Because of its high iron content, parsley is thought to strengthen the blood. It also has high quantities of vitamin C and is therefore a healthy herb to use as a vegetable. Parsley also freshens the breath and is a must-have with garlic bread!

ROSEMARY (*Rosmarinus officinalis*) (perennial)

About rosemary

Rosemary is steeped in folklore, myths and legends. At various times in history it has been burned

ward off evil spirits; the smoke has been inhaled
to cure colds, and there are many fairy stories
associated with it. Rosemary has also been used
in blessings and ceremonies such as baptisms and
weddings.

Rosemary has been cultivated in kitchen gardens
for centuries and is a herb nearly always seen in
herb gardens. One of the great advantages of rosemary is that it is a hardy perennial and will last
for up to twenty years with just a little care and
attention.

It is an evergreen plant with leaves resembling
pine needles, which can be chopped and used in
recipes, although many cooks simply add a sprig of
rosemary to the cooking dish.

Although originally from Mediterranean areas,
rosemary becomes hardier the farther north it trav-
els. It can be used throughout the year and will stay
green even in cold winters.

Properties

1 tbsp Rosemary (1.7g)

Vitamin C	Calcium	Iron	Calories
0.4mg	0.5mg	0.11mg	2

Growing

Rosemary can be grown from seed although it isn't
always easy to germinate. The best way to get a
rosemary plant started is the cutting method.

Rosemary.

Rosemary leaves.

Rosemary likes a sunny and sheltered spot. The plant should be positioned in a place where strong winds can't damage it. It will last through most cold winters but wind and rain along with low temperatures could kill the plant.

From seed

If you are trying your hand at sowing rosemary seed, sow all the seed you have and have plan B ready to go! Start the seed in trays or pots of seed compost. They must be well drained. Keep the surface of the compost moist but never waterlogged. Seed can take up to three months to germinate. The pots or trays need to be kept warm until seed-lings are ready to plant out. Sowing from seed is not the usual form of propagating rosemary, and recommended growing instructions on the seed packet may give some extra tips to getting a good germination rate.

When the plants are large enough to handle they can be transplanted into the garden or containers. Rosemary is happy to grow in containers, although the plants do grow fairly large so a spacious pot is required.

Rosemary has been known to tolerate near-drought conditions but it needs water during hot, dry periods to thrive. Watering will keep it growing and usable for longer in the year.

It's unlikely that you'll need more than a couple of good, well-established rosemary plants, but they are attractive and don't take up much time or space so it's worth thinking about planting a few extra. If you are tight for space though, just get one or two plants thriving and it will be plenty. As with all herbs, rosemary likes to be used.

Cuttings

Although you may only want one or two rosemary plants, when you plant cuttings, allow a few more as some may not take. You can simply cut branches from an existing plant and push into a well-dug area of soil, or into a container. The most successful way to propagate rosemary is to take 8 to 10cm (3 to 4in) cuttings just above or below a leaf joint from a healthy plant. Then push the cuttings into pots of potting compost. Keep the pots warm – use a propagator if you have one. Or simply cover the pots with plastic until the roots have established.

The cuttings will take about two months to grow roots and they should then be carefully transplanted into the garden or larger containers. Position in sunny spot.

In a region with mild winters, a seedbed is a good area to get cuttings started. The soil is usually fine and more maintained than other parts of the garden. Wherever you plant the cuttings make sure the ground is well drained and protect from extreme cold.

Rosemary tolerates fairly poor soil, but doesn't particularly like acidic soil. Add a little lime to the ground before planting out if the soil in your garden is particularly acidic.

Storing

As rosemary is an evergreen, it is available fresh all year round, but in rare cases it can be dried. Hang sprigs up inside a paper bag to collect the needles as they fall. Drying will reduce the strength of the flavour and scent.

Medicinal uses for rosemary

Rosemary leaves are used in an infusion to soothe digestive problems, stress, headaches and a number of other ailments. The oil is used externally for insect bites and is also widely used in the cosmetic industry. Rosemary leaves can be added to a bath to relax nerves and tension. Sew some into a small muslin bag and hang from the tap while the water is running.

SAGE (*Salvia officinalis*) (perennial)

About sage

Sage originates from southern Europe and although it is a hardy perennial, it should be replaced approximately every five years.

To the Ancient peoples, sage was considered to be a herb of wisdom, good health and psychic powers, among other things. In medieval times it was grown to drown urban smells, and the Romans believed it to be the herb of immortality.

It was used in medicinal preparations to treat infections, memory loss, fever and stomach problems. Sage has been used medicinally for thousands of years and has been used to flavour food for a similar amount of time.

Sage originated in the Mediterranean but is now widely grown. There are many varieties available including variegated types grown for decorative, as well as culinary, purposes.

Sage is mostly grown for culinary use but is still used by herbalists and alternative remedy enthusiasts, with good results.

Sage.

Properties

1 tbsp ground dried sage (2g)

Vitamin C	Calcium	Iron	Calories
0.6mg	33mg	0.56mg	6

Growing

It is more satisfying to grow sage from seed, but you will have to wait over a year before using it. Alternatively you can buy small, ready-grown plants from a

Variegated sage.

because there are a number of different varieties and some may suit your region better than others. Growing sage from seed usually allows more choice, and there is no reason why you shouldn't grow a number of different varieties. Variegated types will add a touch of colour and design to either a herb garden or vegetable patch.

Layering

Sage is propagated most often by layering. Because it is a woody shrub, the stem will produce roots. Layer from mature, well-established plants, in the spring or autumn. Peg lower stems down and cover with about half an inch of soil. Water and leave to grow roots. Once the plant is firmly established, the layered stem can be cut and the new plant transplanted if required.

Cuttings

Take 8 to 10cm (3 to 4in) cuttings from a well-established plant in spring and summer, and push them into a container of potting compost – make sure it is well drained. Keep warm and watered but not too moist. The containers or pots should be kept in a sheltered spot, away from wind or frost pockets. Once the cuttings have taken root and are starting to grow, they can be transplanted into larger containers or out into the herb garden.

Sage doesn't need a lot of watering or maintaining. Later in the year, when the flowers have died back, the plants can get straggly. Prune back to the shape you want them. Early summer is usually the best time as sage flowers in the spring, although flowering times can vary with different varieties. There are new hybrids that have beautiful foliage but are reluctant to flower. Make sure you know which type you are buying.

Sage is a fairly hardy plant and will survive most winters, although they may not survive a very long cold spell. The plants will suffer if the roots are too wet. Containers are a good idea if you have particularly cold, wet winters. Bring the containers in before the first frosts and keep them indoors until spring.

Sage thrives in well-drained soil in a part sun/part shade position. A walled herb garden is ideal. Plant some near rocks or in a rockery. Kept trimmed sage will grace the rock garden for years.

nursery or garden centre, or start your plants from cuttings.

From seed

Sow your seed in early spring in seed trays or pots of new compost. Keep damp but not too wet and make sure the containers are well drained. Sage is native to Mediterranean regions and doesn't need a lot of watering.

Put plants out into their permanent positions a bit later in the year and keep protected. Check the growing recommendations on your seed packet

Storing

ome sage flower varieties can be picked in spring nd candied. The leaves can be dried and stored n sealed jars. Hang stems or lay on racks until dry nough to crumble before storing. Remember to bel the jar. The leaves can also be frozen and ealed in freezer bags. In milder climates, sage can e picked fresh for most of the year.

Medicinal uses for sage

age has been used in medicinal preparations or centuries and is commonly known today to educe menopausal night sweats. Sage has volatile ils, which can be transformed into very effective nedicinal aids; however, the oils do contain toxins o sage should never be taken in large doses.

THYME (*Thymus vulgaris*)
(perennial)

About thyme

'hyme is a fairly hardy perennial, and will last in our herb garden for several years. It is easily prop-gated and has been cultivated in kitchen gardens or centuries. It has been used in food prepara-tion and in particular the preserving of meat, since Roman times. Originating from Mediterranean areas, it will tolerate dry conditions.

Thyme has also been the main ingredient in many medicinal preparations and is known to soothe coughs and colds, as well as to cure a number of other minor ailments.

There are myths and legends attached to thyme, proving that over the centuries it has always played an important part in everyday life. One such belief was that if a woman wore thyme in her hair she would attract a husband.

Thyme is certainly sweet smelling and is invalu-able in a kitchen. It should be added early in cook-ing because it is slow to release its flavours. It is also very effective as a quick cure for the common cold.

There are a number of different varieties of thyme but the garden thyme *(thymus vulgaris)* and the lemon scented thyme *(thymus x citriodorus)* out-strip most other types for taste and smell.

Properties

1 tsp fresh thyme (0.8g)

Vitamin C	Calcium	Iron	Calories
1.3mg	3mg	0.14mg	1

hyme.

Purple-flowered thyme.

Growing

Thyme can be started from seed, cuttings or root division. Once your plants are established, use as much as you can. It is a useful herb both medicially and in the kitchen. Cut short stems and rub off the leaves with a blunt knife or between your fingers.

From seed

Growing your own seed is very satisfying, but it will be a while before you can use the leaves. Sow seed in early spring in trays or pots of seed compost and plant outside later in the year, when the plants are strong enough. Check on your seed packet for growing recommendations.

Thyme seed can be directly sown into the garden around May, as long as all danger of frost has passed. Sow in shallow drills about 30cm (12in) apart and water. Keep weed-free and watered until germination. Don't over-water thyme. It prefers a dry environment, but the seed will need some water to germinate.

Thin the young plants as they come up, leaving space for the others to grow into. Thyme likes space to grow and makes a good ground cover for small patches in the garden. The plants removed from the line can be re-planted or potted up.

Don't use any leaves in the first year of growth. Let the plant become established and produce strong roots.

Thyme should be placed in a sunny and fairly dry place in the garden if possible. It is happy to grow in containers and will thrive near a rockery, raised herb garden, or on a stone wall. The soil must be well drained. Water occasionally, but never let the ground become too wet. Thyme likes a light soil. If your soil is heavy, mix some sand in before planting.

Root division

Thyme needs to be divided every three or four years when the plant becomes woody and straggly. Dig up carefully and pull the roots apart. Choose the healthiest looking pieces and re-plant around the garden or in pots. Thyme potted up in a pretty container makes a lovely gift.

Cuttings

Thyme can be started from cuttings. Cut fresh stems from an established healthy plant in the spring. Push the cuttings into potting compost and water. Keep the pots in a warm, sunny place, preferably indoors or sheltered from cold and wind if outside. Water occasionally but don't let the soil become too wet. Make sure the pots are well drained. The following year, plant out the cuttings that have developed roots and are starting to grow more leaves.

In very cold winters, when temperatures drop to 10°F or below, a mulch will protect the roots from freezing.

Storing

Thyme is better used fresh but can be dried by hanging stems upside down in paper bags, or laying on trays in a bright and airy place until the leaves can be crumbled. Store in a sealed jar and label. Stems can be frozen as well. Pick as the flowers are starting to appear and freeze quickly.

Medicinal uses for thyme

Thyme is a well-known cure for common cold symptoms. Steep fresh leaves in boiling water, allow to cool and drink. Add a dash of lemon juice or honey for extra effect. Thyme is a natural antiseptic and is a good quick cure for cuts and scrapes in the garden.

CHAPTER 6

Twenty Occasional Herbs

The following occasional herbs are just as easy to grow as the everyday herbs in Chapter Five, but some of them need just a little extra tender loving care. All of them have either culinary or medicinal uses, if not both:

- Aloe Vera
- Angelica
- Blackberry
- Borage
- Burdock
- Caraway
- Chamomile
- Chervil
- Comfrey
- Daisy
- Dandelion
- Dog Rose
- Echinacea
- Feverfew
- Savory
- Sorrel
- Tarragon
- Violet
- Watercress
- Yarrow

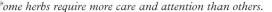

Some herbs require more care and attention than others.

ALOE VERA (*Liliaceae*)
(perennial)

About aloe vera

Historical evidence suggests that aloe vera originated in Africa although it is now grown in many countries. In moderate climates, aloe is often grown as a houseplant and thrives well in containers. It will grow happily in humid conditions as long as the roots aren't in water. The plant will tolerate very high temperatures, as well as very cold air temperatures, but low ground temperatures will damage the roots.

The use of aloe vera in medicinal preparations has been recorded for more than 2,000 years. The

Aloe vera.

sap from the leaf of the plant is a thick gel and it is this gel that holds all the healing ingredients that aloe vera is becoming progressively well known for. There is a wide commercial trade in aloe vera and it has proved to cure many minor ailments as well as some chronic conditions.

The plant is 95% water and is therefore frost tender. It is normally grown indoors as a houseplant in the United Kingdom and similar climates. In warmer climates aloe can be grown outside in full sun or very light shade.

Properties

The gel inside aloe vera leaves consists of many vitamins and minerals, including vitamins A, C and B12. It also contains twenty of the twenty-two amino acids required by a human body and is therefore an excellent aid to healing. It is a very useful herb to have in the home.

Growing

Aloe vera has become very popular in recent years and is available in the form of ready-grown plants from many garden suppliers. Plants should be kept on a sunny windowsill and kept indoors for most of the year. During warm summer months, pots ca[n] be put outside during the day. Don't forget to brin[g] them in before the temperature drops.

From seed

Aloe vera can be grown from seed although it ca[n] take anything from one to six months to germinate[.] It must be kept warm during this time. It shoul[d] be started in well-drained trays or pots of warm[,] fresh compost and kept damp. Water gently bu[t] regularly.

When the plants are large enough to handle[,] prick out carefully into individual pots and kee[p] warm. Position in a sunny spot, either in a green[-] house or on a windowsill. If you are planting out[-] side choose the sunniest spot in the garden, awa[y] from draughts and frost pockets. Protect with [a] cloche or other cover during the night until th[e] plant has become established, and during the nex[t] cold season. Remember aloe vera is a tropica[l] plant and likes warm humid weather and plent[y] of sun.

Aloe vera leaves.

Offsets

The quickest way to propagate aloe is to take the offsets from the main plant and re-pot immediately using new compost and a container that can be positioned in the sun. Offsets should be 8 to 10cm (3 or 4in) in height and removed carefully so as to minimize damage to the mother plant. All pots and containers should be very well drained. Add extra sand or gravel to compost before planting. Water immediately after planting and then let the soil dry out almost completely before watering again. Use the offsets as they become large enough to remove from the plant to produce new plants. Give them away if you have too many.

During the summer months, aloe vera should be watered well and then left to dry out completely before watering again. During the winter months, the plant rests and requires very little water. When the soil is completely dry add a cup or two of water. The plant (like a cactus) is a succulent, so it holds a lot of water within the leaves and roots, and will rot if watered too much and too often.

Re-potting

The plant will need re-potting every year or so, depending on the size of the pot, how well it grows, and also the quality of the original compost.

Aloe vera has shallow, wide-spreading roots and it should be re-potted into a container that is wider but not necessarily deeper than its current one. Always use fresh compost when re-potting and mix in some sand to help with the drainage.

Storing

Aloe Vera is an evergreen succulent and should be available for use all year round. The gel inside the leaves can be stored and is widely processed in aloe vera preparations. However, in commercial processing, it is usual to use the whole leaf as it is more cost effective. The outer part of the leaf doesn't have any particular medicinal value.

Medicinal uses for aloe vera

The medicinal uses for aloe vera are well documented and various. One particular benefit is a treatment for burns – the sap in the leaves can be applied directly to a minor burn. It aids the body in its healing process and the wound will be much relieved. The sap also relieves pain from stinging insects and plants.

An interesting feature of aloe vera plants is that they continue to release oxygen and absorb carbon dioxide at night, which makes them suitable plants to keep in the bedroom.

ANGELICA (*Angelica archangelica*) (biennial)

About angelica

Angelica, historically, has always been associated with religion. During times of plague, it was believed to have arrived from an angel to protect

Angelica.

mankind from diseases as well as delivering him from evil and providing protection from witchcraft. In the middle ages, angelica root was thought to cure a number of medical conditions. The roots and seeds were burned in the home to freshen air. Generally it was considered to be the most important of all the medicinal herbs.

In Germany, angelica is often carried in processions; the origins of this go back so far that the true meaning behind this tradition has been lost. The symbolic significance of the herb was even recognized in pagan times, before Christianity came into being.

Angelica originated in northern countries but has become naturalized in the United Kingdom and other parts of Europe. It is now a common garden herb. Although normally classified as a biennial, angelica will keep growing for many years in the right environment.

The stem of the plant is most used in sweet desserts or candies and the leaves can be used in salads.

The plant can cause skin allergies and care should be taken when handling it. Wear protective gloves if you are prone to skin problems.

NB: If you collect herbs from the wild extra care should be taken, as angelica is very similar in appearance to hemlock, which is highly poisonous.

Properties

There are many active ingredients found in angelica including useful volatile oils. However, large doses can have an adverse effect on the nervous system, and should not be taken by pregnant women or those suffering from diabetes.

Growing

Angelica can grow up to 2m (7ft) high and should be positioned to the back of a herb garden. It is a biennial plant but if allowed to mature, it will re-seed itself in some areas, and an angelica patch can be productive for many years before the plant needs replacing, if at all. Some growers prefer to restrict the plant from flowering to strengthen the root structure. This encourages the plant to become perennial rather than biennial.

Angelica can be grown in pots.

Angelica is very pest and disease resistant an rarely suffers any problems. The most importar thing with angelica is not to let it dry out. It enjoy a moist soil, although it must be well drained. will also cope with heavy clay soil. Angelica attract wildlife and will help encourage the right insects t pollinate all your garden herbs or vegetables.

All in all, angelica is a very easy and practic plant to have in the herb garden.

Growing from seed

Seed should be planted as soon as possible afte ripening, normally late August to early Septembe

Seed can be started in the spring but the germination rate will be lower.

Collect seed from an existing plant and sow in trays or pots of new potting compost. Keep in a cold frame or greenhouse until the following spring. Trays and pots should be kept away from cold draughts and the soil must be kept damp. If the compost dries out for any length of time before germination, it is unlikely the seed will survive. When the seeds have germinated and the plants are large enough to handle, prick out into individual, well-drained pots of new compost, and keep the pots in a greenhouse or conservatory through the winter.

Put the individual plants out into the garden in spring or after the last frost, in their permanent position. Angelica grows very tall – up to 2m (7ft) high – and should be positioned behind lower-growing plants.

Root cuttings

Angelica can be propagated from pieces of root from a well-established plant. Dig up the plant carefully to avoid damage and re-plant the pieces as soon as possible after digging up. Spring is probably the best time to do this, although if there is someone local to you who grows angelica it is well worth asking their advice, as every region will have a slightly different growing season.

Angelica thrives in a well-drained sunny spot but is happy to grow in partial shade, and will even grow well in light woodland areas. In very hot summers, the midday sun can burn leaves and damage plants, even the sun-loving ones. Water in the morning during the summer months to help protect the leaves and roots from drying out.

Harvest angelica stems when they are young and tender for use in the kitchen.

Storing

Leaves can be dried by tying into small bunches and hanging in an airy, dark place. The stem of angelica is often candied and used in cake decoration. Tea can be made from bruised roots although the roots are poisonous if eaten fresh. Seeds don't store well and should be used as soon as possible after harvesting.

Medicinal uses for angelica

An infusion made from the bruised root of angelica can relieve bronchial symptoms. It is also a useful herb to aid digestive problems, reduce flatulence and as a general appetite stimulant. Because of the plants high sugar content it is not considered advisable for diabetics to take in medicinal form.

BLACKBERRY (*Rubus fructicosus*)
(crown is perennial, stems are biennial)

About blackberry

The black fleshy fruit of the bramble plant has been picked and eaten for over 2,000 years, but it wasn't cultivated in the home garden until very recently. Brambles grow wild in a number of regions across the world and the thorns prevent the plant being damaged by grazing wildlife. Birds, however, can use thick bramble growth as protection.

Blackberry plants, more often called brambles, can take over a whole area of land if not checked, although they won't necessarily produce a lot of fruit. Cultivating blackberries is a relatively new idea, as the plant has grown wild for centuries. However, hedgerows and natural habitats have died out over recent years and it is well worth cultivating

Blackberries.

Blackberry fruits are rich in antioxidants.

blackberries in your back garden. New hybrid varieties are worth buying if you want to have blackberries available but don't want the thorns. These plants are far more practical in a home garden, although any wild variety of blackberries can be trained and kept in order with a little maintenance.

The leaves and fruit of the bramble are both useful. They are high in vitamin C content as well as being delicious. The leaves can be used to make teas to help aid recovery from many minor ailments.

Properties

Blackberry fruits are rich in antioxidants and have a high vitamin A and C content. These fruits are one of the highest-ranking fresh foods for nutrition and health benefits. The leaves are also rich in vitamin C.

Growing

Anyone who has ever taken over a piece of unused or neglected land or garden area is sure to understand the strength of the bramble plant. If you are facing a bramble patch and wondering what to do with it, consider training the vines and controlling their growth by clipping back when the plant gets too straggly. Arm yourself with protective clothing and a strong pair of secateurs or shears for this job.

Blackberries are one of the few fruits that will develop and mature in shade. The plants will produce fruit even in the deepest shade, in dense woodland and even behind a garden shed – although perhaps the fruits will not be quite as large or grow as quickly as plants that are getting some sunshine. To produce the best berries choose a sunny and partial shade position if the space is available in the garden.

Blackberries can be started from seed, although many growers prefer to leave this to the experts, as seed can be difficult to germinate. Generally canes are used to propagate the plants.

From canes (cuttings)

Canes can be bought or obtained from a local grower, and care should be taken when positioning them. Blackberry plants can last for fifteen years and will need a permanent patch to thrive, and produce healthy leaf and fruits. To take cuttings from an established plant, simply cut the stems after the last fruits have been harvested and re-plant in a seedbed for the winter until roots have developed. Plant out in the following spring. If a long hot summer is expected, it may be better to leave the cuttings until the following autumn before planting out into their final position.

Because blackberry plants are hardy and flower quite late in the season, there is never a problem with frost. The ground shouldn't be waterlogged but moisture is necessary, so a damp spot in the garden is ideal. Dig over the planting area in the summer before and incorporate plenty of organic matter, well-rotted compost and so on. This will help keep the moisture in the ground. Never plant blackberry canes in waterlogged soil.

The best time to plant your canes is in the autumn but as long as the ground isn't frozen, they can be planted anytime up until the following spring. Allow about 46cm (18in) between plants, although it is advisable to check on the growing recommendations that should be supplied with your canes when you buy them. Hybrid varieties can vary in size and space required.

Plant firmly and water. As long as the ground is damp, canes won't need watering at all. Some hybrids may require watering during a dry spring and summer.

Layering

Propagate more plants by layering in September or when the last of the fruits have been harvested. Choose a low growing, healthy looking branch from a well-established plant and peg to the ground where it is comfortable and not straining either the branch or the mother plant. Push the plant into the earth about 15cm (6in) deep and leave until the next spring before digging up to re-plant.

Dig up carefully, and cut the branch between the mother plant and the new one. Re-plant immediately.

Fruits from the blackberry plant have perhaps the highest source of fibre of all fruits. They are 'multiple' berries and contain more nutrition than many other fresh foods. The fruits will start green, turn red and then eventually a rich purple/black colour. They are fully ripe when they are black and fall off the stem at the slightest touch.

Storing

The blackberry fruit is best eaten fresh on the day it is picked although they will keep in a fridge for three or four days. Blackberries can be frozen but lose some of their texture and taste. Cooking the fruit in a pie, for example, before freezing will help camouflage the poorer taste or texture. A juice can be made from the fruits and stored in sealed jars or frozen in ice cube trays.

The young leaves can be dried. Hang in small bunches until crisp enough to crumble. Store in glass jars and label.

Medicinal uses for blackberry

Blackberries have been used to aid digestion, help reduce symptoms of colds and fevers and as a general tonic since earliest times. A tea made from young leaves is high in vitamins and acts as a tonic to the system. The fresh fruits are packed with fibre and vitamins and should be incorporated into the diet whenever possible.

BORAGE (*Borago officinalis*)
(annual or sometimes biennial)

About borage

Borage was always believed to be the herb of courage and was given to soldiers before going into battle. As well as courage, the herb bestows a general good feeling and is often added to alcoholic drinks and summer punches. It has been used for centuries as a feel-good herb, and is said to alleviate depression.

In Roman times much was recorded about borage and right through to the middle ages the flowers were added to salads. The leaves and flowers were used in cordials. In recent years, borage hasn't been so widely used but it is a wonderful plant to have available.

It is an annual herb, although can sometimes be biennial, growing to about 92 to 122cm (3 or 4ft) in height. It produces beautiful, star-shaped bright blue flowers that attract bees and other wildlife.

The flowers are most often used in decorating sweet dishes such as celebration cakes and the young leaves are used in salads. The stem and larger leaves can be cooked as a vegetable. The leaves have a slight cucumber taste making it a refreshing herb to have in the herb garden.

Properties

100g of raw leaves and stems

Vitamin C	Calcium	Iron	Calories
35.0mg	93mg	3.30mg	21

Borage.

Growing

Being an annual plant, borage is usually grown from seed although the roots can be divided or cuttings can be taken. It is a hardy plant and will re-seed itself and take over the garden if not checked. Borage likes full sun but will grow happily in partial shade.

If the weather is warm enough, borage will tolerate very poor soil and fairly dry conditions, but ideally the soil should be fairly rich and damp to produce bigger, healthier plants. Borage can grow up to 92 or 122cm (3 or 4ft) in height so should be positioned at the back of a bed to avoid over-shadowing lower growing plants.

From seed

Dig over a well-drained area of ground in early spring and incorporate lots of well-rotted manure or compost. Remove any perennial weeds and non-organic debris. Borage seed can be sown in late spring directly outside or later on in the year. Check on your seed packet for growing recommendations for your area. Annual plants can be sown as early in the spring as possible after all danger of frost has passed or the seeds are protected with a cloche. Warm up the soil a little with a cloche for a few days before sowing.

Rake over the area to a fine tilth and then scatter seed fairly sparsely. Cover the seed with a thin layer of soil and water using a watering can with a rosette to avoid washing the seed away. The seed can also be sown in shallow drills in fine soil.

Keep the area weed-free and thin out the seedlings when they are large enough to handle. Allow about 38cm (15in) between plants. Pull out the weaker plants when the soil is damp to avoid damage to the remaining plants.

Borage doesn't transplant well so should always be sown in situ.

Root division or cuttings

Root division or cuttings should be taken in early spring or late summer and replanted as soon as possible. Place 8 to 10cm (3 to 4in) cuttings in their permanent position and protect from extreme temperatures during the winter. Root division isn't generally as successful because borage is predominantly an annual plant. However, in the right conditions, it will self-seed every year. A borage patch can easily become invasive and should be checked regularly for take-over bids on your other herbs.

Borage likes a rich damp soil, and should be watered regularly in dry periods. A spot in the semi-shade will keep the moisture in the ground longer, and borage will thrive there as long as it gets some sun every day.

When in flower, borage is a spectacular plant and shouldn't be hidden away in the garden. Use the flowers to dry and add colour to pot-pourri mixtures. Float fresh flowers on bowls of punch or decorate cakes with them.

Young leaves can be added to salads and large leaves can be steamed or boiled like spinach.

Storing

Borage leaves can be dried. Hang in small bunches in a dark, airy place then crumble and store in a sealed jar and label. Leaves can be dried using a home dryer or very slowly in the oven. Leave the door ajar and turn from time to time. Flowers can be made into syrups and candied for cake decorations.

Medicinal uses for borage

Borage has anti-inflammatory properties and is often used in treating colds and chest complaints. Natural healers use it in remedies for balancing the metabolism and to alleviate menopausal symptoms. It is also the herb of courage and is added to alcoholic drinks and cordials to encourage the feel-good factor.

Burdock seeds.

BURDOCK (*Arctium lappa*)
(biennial)

About burdock

Burdock is one of the plants you may often come home from a walk with, although you may not realise until you take your outer garments off. It has sticky burrs, the fruit of the plant, which adhere to clothes readily. Burdock was the original inspiration for the invention of Velcro.

The herb is prolific in the wild and is rarely grown in the home garden. It will self seed and take over if not checked. However, burdock is a useful herb to grow. It is a large and somewhat unruly plant but can be cultivated and kept under control in a herb garden.

NB: If collecting roots from the wild, extra care must be taken as the roots of deadly nightshade are very similar to burdock.

Burdock is native to Europe and North America but is now grown in many other parts of the world.

Medicinally, burdock is a traditional herb and has been used throughout the centuries for any number of conditions, from hair loss to digestive problems. The ancient Greeks were one of the first to record its attributes and it is still used today by modern herbalists.

Dandelion and burdock has been a popular, commercially made drink in the United Kingdom for many years and is made from fermented dandelions and the root of the burdock plant.

Properties

100g of raw skin, tips and roots

Vitamin C	Calcium	Iron	Calories
3.0mg	41mg	0.80mg	72

Growing

Burdock grows freely in the wild but if you choose to cultivate it at home, it can be started from seed in the spring or autumn.

From seed

Burdock prefers a position in the full sun but will tolerate part shade. Generally, plants grow up to over 1m (4ft) tall and should be positioned at the back of a bed to avoid lower growing plants being overshadowed. Some varieties are even taller.

Dig over the ground quite deeply. Burdock is predominantly a root crop and the ground should be as clean as possible up to about 60cm (2ft) in depth. Remove all perennial weeds, non-organic debris and large stones. Dig in some well-rotted manure or compost in the season before planting. Burdock likes a fairly rich soil, but any unrotted material will cause deformation of the root crop.

In the spring rake over the ground to a fine tilth and sow burdock seed about half an inch deep in lines about 60cm (2ft) apart. For autumn sowings, seed should be sown slightly deeper. Check on your seed packet for growing recommendations in your area. Tamp down the soil with the back of a rake or trowel over the lines of seed and then water well.

The burdock plant.

When your plants are about 15cm (6in) high thin to allow about 15cm (6in) of growing space between them. Do this when the ground is damp or wet so the seedlings can be removed easily without disturbing the others. Pull out the weaker plants.

If you are growing burdock for the root crop only, leaves should be pruned regularly to encourage the plant to strengthen and produce larger roots. Young leaves can be used as a green vegetable and can be picked as soon as the plant is thriving.

Pick off flowers as they appear, to promote more growth. One or two plants could be allowed to flower, for the seed. Burdock usually flowers in late summer and fruits in the autumn. The fruit is the burr, which houses the seed.

The roots take over three months to mature and ˌme burdock varieties will take longer. There are ˌbrids available that will produce roots up to four et in length.

Dig up spring-sown plants in the autumn, or hen the roots are 30 to 60cm (1 to 2ft) long. Use fork and ease the soil away from the plant gently ˌ as not to damage the root. Do this when the soil damp or wet.

ˌtoring

ˌollect the burrs when they are dry and stick to ˌur clothes. Shake out the seeds for storing. Roots ˌn be stored in a fridge for about a week and they ˌn be sliced thinly and dried.

Young leaves can be dried and should be laid out ˌ the sun until crisp. Crumble and store in sealed ˌs and label.

Medicinal uses for burdock

The roots, leaves and seed are used widely in medicinal preparations for many varied conditions. Burdock is known to be an effective treatment for skin conditions as well as being helpful in reducing symptoms of the menopause. Generally the root is used in tinctures and poultices. The bruised leaves can soothe swellings and bruises.

CARAWAY (*Carum carvi*)
(biennial)

About caraway

Caraway tends to be underrated as a garden herb. Although it is native to many regions, including Europe and Asia, it is only grown in a few places commercially and then mostly for the seed. The leaves and roots of caraway are also edible and it has been said that caraway roots, which are slightly smaller than parsnips, are tastier than many root

ˌaraway.

vegetables. The leaves can be used in salads and soups, and taste similar to dill.

Caraway is in the same family as parsley and grows to about 30cm (1ft) tall in the first year and then up to 60cm (2ft) in the second before it produces seed. It is often found growing on wasteland.

Caraway is one of the herbs that can be used in sweet or savoury dishes. The seed has been traditionally used to flavour bread and cakes, as well as pickles, cabbage, cauliflower and cheese.

Records of caraway being used as a medicinal and culinary herb go back thousands of years. It is an easy herb to grow, although it can become slightly invasive, and is an excellent choice for a herb garden.

Caraway leaves.

Properties

1 tsp (2.1g) of seed

Vitamin C	Calcium	Iron	Calories
0.4mg	14mg	0.34mg	7

Growing

Garden suppliers don't always stock ready-grow caraway plants, although it is possible to find then The best way to start your herbs is by sowing see

From seed

Seed should be started directly in the prepare bed as caraway has taproots and doesn't transplar

ell. Choose a sunny well-drained spot and dig the round over well. Dig fairly deep, especially if you ant the roots to grow to full maturity. Remove ny non-organic debris, large stones and perennial eeds to give the plants a good start. Make sure e soil is fairly light. Caraway has a long taproot nd growth will be stunted in heavy clay soils. Dig some sand if necessary.

Rake the surface over to a fine tilth and sow the ed in lines about 30cm (12in) apart. Cover with ery little soil and water gently. Keep weed-free nd watered. Caraway tends to germinate fairly usily.

Seed can be sown in spring or late summer to utumn. Spring sowings will flower the following ear but the leaf is available for use throughout the rst year. Autumn sowings will flower in late summer the following year.

Autumn sowings from seed recently ripened ften germinate better than seed kept until the following spring. However, if the winter is likely to e cold in your region, it's advisable to protect the edlings over the winter months with a cloche or old frame.

Caraway has delicate lacy foliage but can sometimes be mistaken for weeds. Generally, it won't row to more than 30cm (12in) high during the rst year and weeds tend to grow taller. When the ants are large enough to handle, they should be inned out to allow about 20cm (8in) between ch plant. Hoe gently from time to time to remove ny weeds.

As the plant grows, leaves can be picked regularly. This will help develop more root growth. uring the second year of growth, caraway will roduce less foliage but will grow flowers from hich the seed is collected. As the flower heads art to dry, remove them from the plant. If caraay is allowed to self-seed it can become invasive the herb garden, so picking off all the flowers will lve the problem.

During very cold winters, mulch the plants to revent damage to the roots. After the flowers have ed and been removed during the second year, the ot can be dug up and eaten as a vegetable similar parsnip.

Generally, caraway is a fairly hardy plant but is ccasionally attacked by caterpillars.

Storing

When flowers are dying, remove from the plant and hang upside down in paper bags to collect the seed. Store seed in a dark glass jar. Light will weaken them. Use them in cakes, bread and other dishes. Leaves are not suitable for storing although young leaves could be hung until crisp enough to crumble. Use as a flavouring in winter soups. Roots are best eaten directly after harvesting but should keep for a couple of days in the fridge.

Medicinal uses for caraway

Although caraway was once considered to be a retaining medication for keeping your loved one, these days it is used chiefly as flavouring. The essential oil of caraway is also known to reduce flatulence and is a mild tonic. It is often used in conjunction with other medications.

CHAMOMILE (*Chamaemelum*) (perrenial)

About chamomile

Two main types of chamomile are widely grown: Roman chamomile (*Chamaemelum nobile*) and

Chamomile flower.

German chamomile (*Matricaria recutita*). Both have similar qualities and are used in similar ways.

Records show that the Egyptians worshipped chamomile and used it in medicinal aids as well as cosmetic preparations. It has been used for centuries all over Europe and was distributed further afield during the sixteenth century.

Its daisy-like flowers make it an attractive addition to a herb garden and, as the plant is perennial, it will grace your garden for many years. Chamomile often grows around the edge of gardens and can be found in the wild. It re-seeds itself readily but is easily controlled. It is often left to grow between paving slabs and alongside pathways. When walked on, the plant releases a pleasant scent.

Chamomile can grow up to a metre (about 4ft) in height but generally it will grow as a shrub around 60 to 90cm (2 to 3ft) high. Hybrid varieties may differ slightly. It makes a good edging plant, especially around a lawn or grassed area.

While only the flowers are used in the home, the whole herb is used in commercial beer making. Chamomile tea is widely drunk as a mild sedative and can be bought in most supermarkets or health shops.

Properties

1 cup (8fl oz) of chamomile tea (brewed)

Vitamin C	Calcium	Iron	Calories
0mg	5mg	0.19mg	2

Growing

Although very rare, there are reports of allergic reactions to chamomile. Care should be taken if you are prone to plant allergies.

Small plants are sometimes available at garden suppliers, but chamomile is easily propagated from seed, which normally germinates fairly quickly.

From seed

Once established in your garden. Chamomile rarely needs re-sowing. In the right conditions it will readily re-seed itself and come up year after year. It can also be grown successfully in pots, which should be well drained but never allowed to dry out. After a

Chamomile leaves.

couple of years in the same pot, the soil may nee feeding with an organic fertilizer or transplanting a bigger pot with fresh compost.

When the plant is in full bloom, chamomile a perfect container plant to enjoy around a sea ing area in the garden. Roman chamomile tends stay as a low growing plant, often only growing about 30cm (12in) high. Check on the seed pack before you buy so you are sure which variety yo are growing. German chamomile grows muc taller and will need to be positioned towards th back of a bed to avoid overshadowing low-growin plants.

Choose a sunny, well-drained spot in the garde As soon as the ground is workable in the sprin, dig over and remove any perennial weeds ar non-organic debris. Whether the ground has bee worked a lot or not at all, dig in some well-rotte compost or organic fertilizer. Rake the ground a fine tilth.

Seeds can be scattered over the prepared are and carefully covered with a light layer of soil. C sow the seed in very shallow drills. Water with spray or rosette attachment on a watering can avoid disturbing the seed.

Keep the area free of weeds and the soil dam but not waterlogged. When the seedlings are lar enough to handle, thin them to about 30cm (12i apart. Again, though, check your seed packet f growing recommendations as some varieties w need more space. When the new plants come u around your main plant in the following year, as no doubt they will, remove them gently and try re-planting them. Water well directly after planting. Or re-plant into pots of fresh new compost. Keep in a sunny spot but don't allow the pots or containers to dry out.

The flowers can be harvested as soon as they are in full bloom and added to salads or used in tisanes. They can also be made into cosmetic and medicinal preparations. Pick flowers gently, and the chamomile plant will produce more blooms throughout the season.

Storing

Chamomile flowers can be dried and stored for several months. Pick when the flowers are in full bloom and lay on trays to dry in the sun or in a very slow oven with the door ajar. The flowers can also be hung in small bunches although there will need to be a short stalk allowed when picking. Hang small bunches in paper bags to collect flowers as they dry.

When the flowers are completely dry, store in a sealed glass jar and keep in a dark place.

Medicinal uses for chamomile

Chamomile has mild sedative properties and has, for many years, been made into a soothing and calming tea. It aids digestion and alleviates symptoms of the common cold. Chamomile is also used in cosmetic preparations including hair lighteners and shampoos.

It has been found useful for reducing joint inflammation such as arthritis and easing menstrual cramps.

CHERVIL (*Anthriscus cerefolium*)
(annual)

About chervil

Chervil is in the same family as carrots and is similar to parsley. There are two main varieties, one with flat and one with curly leaves. It has a taste a little like anise and brings out the flavour of other herbs when cooked with them.

Chervil.

It was once known as 'myrris' because of its resemblance to myrrh. It has been used in religious ceremonies and also has many medicinal qualities.

In Roman times chervil was used as a spring tonic but it is not widely used as a medicinal herb these days. It is mostly used as a culinary herb and is one of the main herbs used in French cuisine as part of the bouquet garni mixture. The other herbs – chives, tarragon and parsley – complement each other and chervil brings out the taste in all of them.

Chervil can be added to many dishes and should not be ignored when the recipe tells you to use chervil (optional). Add some to your recipes and get lots of brownie points for a wonderful tasting meal.

Chervil leaves.

Chervil is native to middle-eastern countries but can be grown easily in many moderate climates.

Properties

1 tsp of dried chervil (0.6g)

Vitamin C	Calcium	Iron	Calories
0.3mg	8mg	0.19mg	1

Growing

Chervil can run to seed very quickly, especially in hot sun, and should be positioned in a partial shade in your garden. Chervil doesn't transplant well and should be started from seed in situ.

From seed

Dig over the soil in early spring, or as soon as the ground is workable. Make sure the area is well drained and gets some shade during the day. Remove any perennial weeds and non-organic debris and rake the soil to a fine tilth.

Sow the seed in drills about 2.5cm (1in) deep and cover gently with soil or compost. Water well. Check on the growing recommendations on your seed packet, but generally the first sowing of chervil can be made in mid-spring. As the plant is notorious for bolting (running to seed), sow a short line of seed every couple of weeks through until midsummer and then another later sowing in late summer for autumn use. In this way, fresh chervil will be available throughout the summer and autumn months.

Keep the young seedlings free from weeds and water in dry weather. Chervil won't transplant easily but will need thinning. To avoid having to throw away too many plants, sow seed as sparsely as possible at each sowing.

Thin plants when they are about 5cm (2in) tall and when the soil is damp. Water the area first necessary. Leave the strongest plants to grow and pull out the weaker ones. Allow about 8cm (3in) of growing space between them. Then thin them again, to about 30cm (12in) apart a few weeks later, again removing the weaker plants.

As long as the soil isn't allowed to dry out and chervil doesn't get too much direct, hot midday sun, the plants will need little looking after. The hardest thing to control with chervil is running to seed. Avoid direct sunlight and water regularly to alleviate the problem as much as possible. Pick leaves regularly and cut off flowering stems before they bloom to encourage more foliage.

As chervil likes part shade, it's ideal for growing indoors in pots on a windowsill. Use well-drained pots of new compost and sow a few seeds in each pot. Keep the compost damp. Remove the weaker seedlings when the plants are about 5cm (2in) tall and leave the strongest plant to grow.

Make sure the pots don't dry out and protect from direct sun through glass. A north-facing windowsill is probably the ideal spot in your home for chervil.

Storing

Fresh chervil leaves will store well in a sealed bag in a fridge for up to a week. Leaves can be dried and should be hung in a dark, airy place preferably in a brown paper bag to avoid dust settling. The leaves can also be dried on racks in the sun. When completely dry, crumble and store in a sealed glass jar and label.

Medicinal uses for chervil

Chervil has been used extensively in folk medicine throughout the ages. It was once said that eating a whole plant cured hiccups. The herb is warm and soothing and is often used as a digestive aid. A cold infusion of chervil tea is effective as an eyewash. Young tender leaves added to salads not only improve the flavour of your meal but are also believed to act as a mild tonic.

COMFREY (*Symphytum officinale*) (perennial)

About comfrey

Although it isn't advisable to medicate yourself with comfrey, it has been used to treat many medical conditions for generations and is still respected in parts of Europe as a healing herb. It is commonly known as 'knitbone' and a poultice of crushed comfrey root is considered to be helpful in relieving injuries such as broken bones. Comfrey is still widely used in the pharmaceutical industry for treating varicose veins and similar conditions.

The comfrey plant is very high in protein – around 33% of the plant is pure protein which is probably responsible for its healing powers.

Comfrey.

Comfrey tea was formerly considered to be helpful in healing many internal injuries, although recent research is pointing to the fact that it can be detrimental to liver function. It is therefore not advisable to take it internally.

Comfrey is often grown as a green manure crop. A small area is planted out with comfrey, harvested at the end of the year and dug into the area to be fertilized. Comfrey is a useful tonic for the soil and helps release nutrients for your plants to absorb. It is grown as an animal feed crop in some parts of the world.

Comfrey is a hardy perennial and will produce leaf after leaf for many years in the right conditions, and will often crop up to three times every year.

Properties

Comfrey is a rare plant source of vitamin B12. It also contains other B vitamins as well as vitamin C and many other useful properties. Comfrey contains mucilage, which is responsible for its well-documented healing action.

Growing

Comfrey is generally grown by crown division, root cuttings or transplant. These methods can all be performed during the summer right up until early autumn.

Crown division

Dig up an established plant gently and pull the crown apart. Re-plant these pieces as soon as possible after digging up, although comfrey is a hardy plant, and should be fine even if left for a day or two.

The soil must be well drained and fairly light. The comfrey plant is a deep-rooted herb and needs depth of soil to thrive. It won't do well in shallow soil.

Comfrey likes some sun but will still grow well in partial shade. It is a good plant to fill up a shady spot in the garden although it can be invasive as the plants get larger and larger every year.

Re-plant the pieces of crown and water in well. Comfrey thrives in a fairly damp soil but it should not be waterlogged. The plant tends to be fairly self-sufficient and has deep roots so will find water where shallow-rooted plants may not. However, regular, gentle watering will help comfrey grow and produce more leaves.

Comfrey is one of the fastest growing herbs and within a few weeks will have produced leaves up to about 30cm (12in) long.

Root cuttings

Again, choose a well-established plant. Dig up carefully and break the root apart. Re-plant the pieces as soon as possible after digging up.

Keep the weeds away for the first year while the plants become established, and then watch it doesn't take over the whole garden!

Comfrey is the best herb to use as a feed for the soil in your garden as well as an animal feed. Chickens, rabbits and other animals will happily eat comfrey leaves, although they should be picked a day in advance. This allows the leaves wilt a little and loose the leaf 'hairs'. Domestic animals will rarely eat fresh comfrey leaves.

Cut down all the leaves before the plant flowers and use as a tonic for the soil in your garden. Lay fresh leaves in the bottom of trenches dug for potatoes. The comfrey leaves release nutrients into the soil, which the potato plants, will take up. Comfrey really can help to increase the quality and quantity of your crops.

Or you can use it to make a liquid tonic. Place comfrey leaves in a tub or barrel with a heavy weight pressing them down. Cover for a few weeks. The resulting liquid can be used to feed tomatoes and other summer fruits and vegetables. The only problem with this is that when you lift the cover off the smell is something like an open sewer. But it is really good for the garden!

Comfrey leaves can be harvested up to three times a year, making it probably one of the most prolific herbs in the garden. It is a very hardy plant and will stick around for years. In very harsh winters mulch could be used to protect the roots from freezing, but normally the plants are strong enough to cope with fairly low temperatures.

Storing

Comfrey can be harvested up to three times a year and therefore doesn't need a lot of storing. The leaves can be dried and stored to make comfrey tea during the winter months, although comfrey should never be taken in large doses. Hang the leaves in a dust-free, dark and airy place until crisp, then crumble them into glass jars and label.

Medicinal uses for comfrey

Comfrey has probably been used as a healing aid for more ailments than any other herb. It is also considered to be an excellent animal feed. Some animals can consume vast quantities of comfrey; however, it has been found that large doses of comfrey can cause liver damage in humans.

Externally, comfrey root can be grated and made into a poultice to treat bruising and swellings. It was used in bygone days to treat broken bones.

Another medicinal use for comfrey is as a treatment for soil; it helps release nutrients for your plants to take up.

DAISY (*Bellis perennis*) (perennial)

About daisies

There are thousands of different species of daisy. Perhaps the most commonly known is the lawn daisy (*Bellis perennis*) which is often considered to be a weed. The common lawn daisy is steeped in myths and legends and was formerly known, in

Daisies.

A daisy flower.

English, as 'day's eye' because the flower opens and closes with the sun.

The daisy is considered to represent innocence and is often associated with children. And as children are always drawn to them, this makes perfect sense! For centuries they have been collected as small posies to give to friends or made into daisy chains to hang around the neck, or decorate the hair.

The daisy has been used as a healing herb for many years and is known as one of the wound herbs. The plant aids in the healing process when applied to a fresh wound.

It is a hardy plant and will turn up uninvited on most lawns at some point. Daisies will start flowering early in the spring and carry on right through until the autumn and in some areas will even produce a flower or two in the winter months. The low, flat leaves of the daisy plant will prevent other plants, weeds and grass from growing, and will stay green all year.

Properties

Daisies are a good source of vitamin C although the leaves can be bitter tasting. The buds, flowers and leaves have healing properties.

Growing

Daisies tend to come up in the garden whether you want them or not. Although considered to be a weed by many gardeners, the daisy is a useful herb to grow and is also a great source of entertainment for children of all ages. Lawn daisies are a hardy plant and can be mown down many times before they are defeated, if at all.

The leaves grow low to the ground and prevent other weeds from growing. If you do need to plant daisies, they can be started from seed.

From seed

There are many different varieties of daisy but the lawn daisy is one of the types considered to be a herb. Look for the seed labelled 'lawn daisies' or *bellis perennis*.

It is also a good idea to obtain fresh seed as they will have a higher germination rate. It is possible to collect the seed in summer and it should be planted immediately if possible.

Choose a sunny spot in the garden if you are preparing a special place for your daisies, although they will tolerate partial shade. Daisies are very hardy plants but they don't thrive well if the soil is too dry or too wet. Make sure the ground is well drained and keep watered during the summer if it dries out too much. Daisies are tolerant of all types of soil; rich, poor, acid or alkaline, which is probably why they have a reputation among gardeners for being a weed.

Dig over the ground and remove any perennial weeds and non-organic debris. Rake over to a fine tilth and sow your seeds in lines. When the plants are large enough to handle, thin to allow growing space of about 10 to 15cm (4 to 6in) for each plant. Check on your seed packet for growing recommendations.

If a very cold winter is expected, sow seed in pots during the autumn or winter months and keep warm and watered. When the ground is workable in the spring, plant out individual plants. Daisies are perennial and will come back every year so choose your spot well in the garden before planting. Other types of daisies can be grown along with the common lawn daisy, although they may not have the same properties and shouldn't be taken internally or used in medicinal preparations unless it is confirmed that the plants are edible on the seed packet.

Many daisies propagate themselves by sending out new growth on runners, like strawberry plants. These can be separated off the main plant and re-positioned. Separate the new plants after they have flowered.

Daisy plants are often available in garden centres and suppliers. Check the variety before you buy.

Storing

Flowers and leaves can be dried but daisies tend to be around for most of the year so can be used fresh as much as possible. Fresh leaves and flowers can be hung in a dark, airy and dust free place until completely dry and stored in sealed jars.

Medicinal uses for daisies

Daisies have been used as a medicinal herb for centuries. Preparations from the flowers are used to relieve mouth ulcers, coughs and colds and also to soothe patients in shock. A daisy tea will relieve the nervous system from stress and a handful of daisy flowers in a bath will melt away all the tensions of the day.

DANDELION (*Taraxacum officinalis*) (perennial)

About dandelion

A whole book could be written on the medicinal properties of the dandelion. Although nearly always considered to be a weed, it is probably one of the most useful herbs grown today, privately as well as commercially. Every part of the dandelion plant can be used for either culinary or medicinal purposes.

The root of the dandelion plant is used as a caffeine-free coffee substitute; the leaves are used

Dandelions.

in salads and can also be cooked like spinach; the flowers can be made into a delicious jam and the stem holds a milky sap which is a wonder cure for warts.

This is really a very useful plant to have in the garden and once there are a few flowers going to seed, there won't be any problem with them coming up year after year.

The common name, dandelion, is a corruption of the French 'dents de lion' meaning lion's teeth. There have been many names, as well as myths, associated with dandelions over the years. One of the better known myths is that children might wet the bed after picking the flowers. There is a grain of truth in this as dandelions are a strong diuretic, although simply picking them doesn't have any effect at all!

Once established in a garden, dandelions can be hard to get rid of, so they must be positioned well, or use them as they come up randomly around the garden, as they surely will. They have a very strong taproot and are difficult to pull out of the soil. A fork or spade is usually needed to dislodge the root. Allowing flower heads to seed will spread the dandelions, which is why gardeners everywhere discourage children from blowing the seed head away.

Properties

100g of raw dandelion leaves

Vitamin C	Calcium	Iron	Calories
35.0mg	187mg	3.10mg	45

Growing

Growing dandelions is not normally considered to be necessary, as they are a prolific weed and will turn up in most gardens at one time or another. However, gardeners have been trying to get rid of the plant for many so years, you may find the dandelion avoids your particular patch of ground. Collecting dandelions from the wild is fine but it is not advisable near roads or farmer's fields, unless it is an organic farm, because of the chemicals presen in the air and soil. Always pick wild dandelion from environmentally friendly areas.

The dandelion really is a very hardy plant. carefully dug up from one place they can be re planted where you want them. Digging up a dan delion plant or two from wasteland can be all yo need to get dandelions established. Always chec before taking plants from the wild. Many area are conserving the wild plant-life and won't tak kindly to someone arriving with a spade and dig ging up their plants, even if they are just dande lions.

From seed

It's not always easy to come by the seed for dande lions although wild flower seed suppliers should b

A dandelion flower.

able to help. Nipping the seed head off a plant and scattering it on your patch is worth a try. The seed head is the 'clock' – that is the white fluffy ball that replaces the flower.

Because dandelions are such a widespread weed, they come up where they are happiest, and they aren't always easy to contain, or indeed germinate in the area you have allocated. However, to give them a good start, dig over the ground and remove any perennial weeds and non-organic debris, then rake over the soil to a fine tilth. Gently scatter the seed and rake over carefully, then water.

Pull out weeds until the dandelion plants are established. After that they will look after themselves, although a little water in hot dry periods helps to keep them growing well.

Use young leaves from established plants to add to salads. They can also be cooked like spinach. The flowers should be harvested as they appear or left to re-seed themselves. Use roots when you have established a healthy dandelion patch. Dig around the plant carefully with a fork and ease the root out of the ground. Dandelion roots tend to be long and deep so will need to be carefully dug out to avoid damaging them. Choose a wet day or water the surrounding area first.

Storing

Dandelion leaves can be dried and kept to add to soups and stews, as well as being used to make herbal teas during the winter. Dandelion flowers make a delicious jam, which can be kept almost indefinitely. The roots are roasted and ground to make a coffee substitute.

Medicinal uses for dandelion

The milky sap inside the stem of the dandelion plant has been successfully used for many years as a treatment for warts and verrucas. The leaves are a good source of vitamin C and iron, and therefore provide a good tonic in the winter months. Make a tea from the dried leaves and, for caffeine reduction, the roasted root makes a warming drink.

DOG ROSE (*Rosa canina*)
(perennial)

About dog rose

The dog rose is one of the wild varieties of the rose family and grows prolifically along hedgerows throughout Europe and elsewhere. Roses have been cultivated for over 2,000 years and are known as the queen of flowers. They need no description although there are over ten thousand cultivated varieties, ranging from climbing roses, shrubs with huge blooms right through to the miniature tea rose.

All of the varieties in the rose family have similar medicinal properties, although the dog rose is highly valued for its prolific growth in the wild

Dog rose.

as well as providing the fruit of the plant known as the 'rose hip'. The rose hip is a good source of vitamin C and is used in cordials and syrups. During the war years, rose hips were picked and used by families all over Europe, especially in the United Kingdom. Rose hip syrup is still considered to be a healthy drink for babies and young children.

Roses are grown commercially for their cut flowers and for many cosmetic and herbal preparations. Rose hip tea is available in many high street supermarkets.

The dog rose grows rapidly and should be allowed quite a large space in the home garden to thrive, although it can be trained to climb over fences and other structures. The plant flowers in early summer and the fruits can be harvested as they become ripe.

Properties

100g fresh rose hips

Vitamin C	Calcium	Iron	Calories
426.0mg	169mg	1.06mg	162

Rose hips.

Growing

Dog rose plants are normally started with cuttings although they can be grown from seed. The seed, however, may take up to two years to germinate. Cuttings can also take about twelve months to grow roots but the rate of successful cuttings is high.

From seed

Because the seed can take up to two years to germinate, the success rate tends to be a bit hit and miss. There are many factors that can lead to the seed not surviving over a long period; lack of heat and/or water, or indeed too much of both. If you are determined to have a go, you should be able to keep the trays in a very warm place and then allow them to cool down periodically. If you sow the seed before it reaches full maturity they can sometimes germinate slightly quicker and may come up in the following spring after autumn sowings. When you buy the seed, check on the manufacturer's growing recommendations before sowing.

Use well-drained seed trays filled with new compost and keep soil moist. When the seedlings are large enough to handle prick them out into individual pots and look after them until they are large enough to plant out in the garden.

Dog rose thrives on a sunny border, that is one next to a low fence or hedge, although it will grow well in partial shade. It can also be trained to grow as a hedge.

From cuttings

Generally roses are propagated from cuttings, and the dog rose is no exception. Prune your plant back in the autumn after the last flowers and fruits have matured and been harvested. Trim the cuttings and select the strongest and healthiest-looking stems to use. Do not use stems that are diseased or damaged.

Cut the pieces you have chosen back to a few inches in length and push them into trays or pots of new compost. Trays should be fairly deep to allow for root growth; pots or containers may be more suitable. Keep the soil damp but not too wet.

Or you can take new shoots from the main plant to propagate more plants. Choose shoots that are about as thick as a pencil and are healthy and free

from damage. Push them into pots of compost and keep fairly damp but not too wet.

Cuttings and shoots can be kept in a cold frame until they have developed roots. Shoots could be ready the following spring, but may not be ready until later in the year. Keep plants until the following year before planting out in the garden, if they haven't established roots by the first spring. Cuttings can also be planted directly outside in a seedbed and moved to their permanent position later on.

Layering

Propagation from layering is also an option with the dog rose. The plant has long, trailing branches and is perfect for this kind of propagation. Choose a low branch that is strong and healthy and peg it to the soil, where it naturally touches the ground, with a u-shaped peg. Cover with a light layer of compost and water well without disturbing the compost. Water in dry periods and keep weeds away.

When the new plant has developed roots it can be cut from the main plant through the layering branch and then re-planted, or left to grow where it is. Cut back the branch remaining on the main plant.

Storing

Dog rose petals can be dried and used in pot-pourri mixtures, although stronger smelling roses are normally used for perfume. Leaves can be dried by hanging in bunches or laying on trays in the sun, then crumbled and stored in a glass jar and used to make tea.

The fruits – the rose hips – should be made into syrups and cordials as soon as possible after harvesting, although they will keep for a day or two before they start to dry out.

Medicinal uses for dog rose

The medicinal uses for all the plants in the rose family have been well documented through the years. The fruits of dog rose – the rose hips – are probably one of the highest sources of vitamin C available, having many times more, weight for weight, than the vitamin C content of oranges and other citrus fruits. A cordial made from rose hips is a natural way to keep colds at bay.

Rose-leaf tea is considered to be a calming drink and the leaves are a good tonic.

ECHINACEA (*Echinacea purpurea*)
(also known as purple cornflower)
(perennial)

About echinacea

Echinacea is known for its many medicinal qualities and is widely used in many ayurvedic, herbal and other natural healing preparations. It was extensively used by native Americans for hundreds, if not thousands, of years. Echinacea is used in vitamin supplements and can be found in most health shops. There is extensive research being done into the medicinal qualities of echinacea and, to date, there seems to be a high success rate with treatments of various ailments.

Echinacea.

The root has traditionally been the part of the herb used in healing and for boosting the immune system as well as for treating colds, as it has antibacterial qualities. But in recent years research strongly suggests that the flowers have healing qualities as well as the roots.

Echinacea is native to mid-western America and was introduced to Europe in the nineteenth century. It likes a sunny spot and will tolerate very dry periods. In a high rainfall region, echinacea is better grown in a greenhouse, windowsill or conservatory, where it can be protected from too much rain. Go for a hot and sunny position and a fairly dry soil and this hardy plant will thrive.

There are a number of different varieties but the purple cornflower (*Echinacea purpurea*) is probably the most widely grown.

Properties

The essential oils, acids and other chemical constituents appear to work together to create Echinacea's healing powers.

Growing

Echinacea can be started from seed or root division. Ready-grown, small plants are often available from garden suppliers. Echinacea likes a fertile soil so if your soil is over-used or hasn't been used at all, dig in some well-rotted manure or organic fertilize before planting.

Because echinacea originates from a hot, dry climate, it won't tolerate too much moisture. If you live in a high rainfall area, the plants will need protecting. Choose a well-drained part of the garden or use a raised bed system with plenty of gravel or sand dug in for drainage. Dig over the ground and remove any perennial weeds and non-organic debris. Rake to a fine tilth.

From seed

Seeds can take up to six weeks to germinate and should be started indoors in the spring, although it's a good idea to check on the growing recommendations on your seed packet for variety and regional differences. Start seeds in well-drained trays of new compost and keep slightly damp and warm unt the seeds have germinated. When the seedlings are strong enough to handle and the ground outside has warmed up, transplant into the garden in a prepared bed. Handle the plants as little and as carefully as possible.

Alternatively, start in pots. Sow a few seeds in each pot and keep indoors or in a warm greenhouse until germinated. When seedlings are a few inches tall or large enough to handle, they need to be thinned. Water the pots well and ease out the weaker plants, leaving the strongest plant in each pot to grow on. Or if they are to be planted out, transplant as soon as they have been taken from the pot. Use degradable pots to avoid damage to the roots. Plant out when the ground has warmed up and isn't too wet.

Echinacea seed can be planted directly in a seedbed outside early in the spring. Again, check on the growing recommendations for your particular variety. The seed should be sown around 5cm (2in) deep and watered very gently. When the seedlings come up, protect from slugs, rabbits and other wildlife. Echinacea shoots are very attractive to garden pests.

Allow around 46cm (18in) of growing room per plant.

Root division

Echinacea is easy to propagate by root division. In spring or late autumn gently dig around the plant and lift the root, being careful not to damage it.

Echinacea flowers.

The root can be pulled apart or cut into separate pieces and re-planted. Each piece of root should be healthy and have fresh shoots. Re-plant quickly and water in. After the plant has been watered in, it should be watered very lightly until signs of new growth appear. As soon as new growth appears and the plant is growing, don't water too often. A well-established echinacea plant shouldn't need watering again until late in the summer, and even then only when the weather is particularly dry. Never plant echinacea in wet ground. If the ground is getting too wet, protect the plant from further rainfall by covering with a large cloche to dry out the surrounding area of soil.

The most important thing about echinacea is that although it is a hardy plant, it won't tolerate too much water.

Echinacea will readily self-seed and produce seedlings around the mother plant every year. These seedlings can be re-planted if necessary. Always allow about 45cm (18in) of growing room. If the new seedlings come up more than 45cm (18in) from the mother plant leave them where they are unless you need the space for another crop.

Harvest the flowers as they bloom, and the roots when the plant has finished flowering and is dormant. When digging up roots, try to limit the disturbance to the surrounding area as the plant may have deposited seeds.

Storing

Seed can be collected from fully matured flower heads. Collect and lay the seed on paper for a couple of weeks until completely dry then store in glass jars for planting next year. Label and keep out of direct light. Roots should be washed then dried using a home dryer or in a very slow oven. When the roots are completely dry they can be stored in a sealed container for up to a year.

Medicinal uses for echinacea

It has been proved that echinacea can help to stimulate the immune system, therefore alleviating colds and flu symptoms. The dried root is traditionally used for medicinal preparations, although research is showing that the flowers contain similar proper-

ties. Echinacea is also known to soothe skin conditions and is added to many herbal preparations and sold as supplements in health shops.

FEVERFEW (*Tanacetum parthenium*) (perennial)

About feverfew

Feverfew is a perennial and fairly hardy herb that grows to about 60cm (2ft) in height. It produces many daisy-like flowers covering the plant throughout the summer months. It is sometimes confused with chamomile but in fact the flowers and leaves are very different.

Feverfew is a well-known cure for headaches and migraines and has been used medicinally for over two thousand years, if not longer. The young leaves can be eaten raw or made into a tea with the flowers. Feverfew is a member of the daisy family and since the 1970s much research has been done on

Feverfew has daisy-like flowers.

his family of plants. All members of the daisy family are known to have many medicinal properties.

Different types of daisy plants, including feverfew, have been used as stewing herbs over the centuries as well as for medications and flavourings. The volatile oils in feverfew are stronger and more pungent than many other herbs and should be used in medicinal preparations with care. The herb is unsuitable for children under two years old, and should not be given to pregnant women as it encourages menstruation. However, it has been used as a successful relaxant in childbirth.

Properties

The main constituent of feverfew, used extensively in treating headaches and migraines, is parthenaloid. All daisy family members contain strong volatile oils and are useful medicinal herbs.

Growing

Feverfew is easily started from seed and should be sown in spring preferably, although some autumn sowings will be successful if the oncoming winter is not too severe or the plants can be protected from the cold. Check the seed packet for growing recommendations for your region. Small, ready-grown plants are usually available in good garden centres or from herb suppliers. Plants can also be started by root division and cuttings.

From seed

Seeds can be sown directly in the garden or in small pots to plant out later. It is also a good plant for container growing and will brighten up a patio with its clusters of daisy-like flowers. Feverfew likes a sunny, well-drained spot in the garden and the ground should be dug over in the spring as soon as it can be worked. Remove any perennial weeds and non-organic debris and dig in some well-rotted manure or organic fertilizer before sowing the seed. Rake the soil over to a fine tilth before planting seed.

The seed can also be started in a seedbed. When the seedlings are large enough to handle, thin to about 5 to 8 cm (2 to 3in) between plants and then later plant them out in their permanent positions. The plants grow to about 60cm (2ft) in height and

Feverfew leaves.

possibly in width also, so should be placed where they will not shade lower-growing plants.

Feverfew is a fairly hardy plant and will establish itself quickly in the herb garden. When the seed germinates and the seedlings are small, watch out for slugs. A pet toad or two should take care of them, or use any other organic method you can to avoid your new plants being eaten. If you buy ready-grown plants from a nursery, plant immediately unless the plants have been started in greenhouse conditions. If they have been cultivated inside, leave them in their pots for a few days. Put them outside during the day and bring them in at night, before planting out to their final position in the garden.

Root division

In late spring or early summer, carefully dig up the plant and, with a sharp spade, cut the root into three or four pieces. Each piece of root should be a good size and healthy with no visible damage. Replant immediately and water in well.

Cuttings

Take cuttings in the autumn. Choose young shoots and cut below a 'heel' in the stem. The heel will give the cutting a better chance of producing roots. By the next spring, the cuttings may be ready to transplant. Transplant when the plant is obviously growing – if you tug the stem gently and it feels as if it is attached to the soil, there is likely to be a good root system already establishing itself. If the cutting slides out of the soil easily then the roots, if any, probably won't be strong enough to plant out to their permanent positions in the garden yet. Wait a few months or until the following spring, keeping the cuttings protected in the winter and watered in the summer, until they have developed roots.

Transplant all new plants to a sunny, well-drained position. Feverfew will die back during the winter months but should come again in early spring. In extremely cold winters a mulch of straw will help protect the roots.

Leaving a few flowers to dry on the plants may result in new seedlings the following year, depending on the winter conditions. Leave these to grow on, or gently lift when they are large enough to handle and transplant.

Storing

As with most herbs, fresh feverfew is stronger in smell and taste. The medicinal qualities are also more effective in fresh leaves. However, leaves can be dried in late summer to keep for the winter months. Dry on racks in the sun, in a home dryer, or hang in small bunches in a dry and dark place until crisp. Crumble into glass jars and label. Store out of direct light.

Medicinal uses for feverfew

The leaves and whole herb are used in medicinal preparations of feverfew. A tincture made from the leaves soothes insect bites and stings externally and can be eaten or drunk as a tisane to treat headaches and migraines as well as being useful as a tonic. It has also been used to soothe nerves.

SAVORY
(Summer savory – *Satureja hortensis*)
(Winter savory – *Satureja montana*)
(Summer savory is an annual and winter savory an evergreen perennial)

About savory

Both summer and winter savory have the same medicinal and culinary properties, although winter

Savory.

savory is coarser and stronger tasting. Both type have been prized for their flavouring over the medicinal qualities for many years, and savory medicinal qualities are well documented.

For thousands of years, savory was used as bo a medicinal and culinary herb, and was cultivate throughout Europe from the ninth century. It native to south-eastern Europe and north Afric but is now widely grown throughout Europe an other parts. It was also used as a love potion f many years and is mentioned throughout history i herbal and medicinal books. Savory is used exten sively in French cuisine and is one of the mixtu of herbs known as bouquet garni.

Summer savory is an annual plant which grow to about 30 to 38cm (12 to 15in) high and ha pale lilac flowers in the summer. Winter savory an evergreen perennial. It grows as a hardy shru and, in milder climates, the leaf can be used rig through the winter months.

Savory is likened to thyme and marjoram for i flavour and appearance.

Properties

(Winter and summer savory have the same proper ties.)

1 tsp (1.4g) of ground spice

Vitamin C	Calcium	Iron	Calories
0.7mg	30mg	0.53mg	4

Growing

Summer savory is raised from seed every year and winter savory can be started from seed, cuttings or root division. Although winter savory is a perennial plant and will keep growing for many years in the right conditions, after a couple of years it will start to become woody and produce less foliage. It is therefore a good idea to replace winter savory every two or three years.

Summer savory from seed

Summer savory likes a sunny position and a fairly rich, light soil. If the soil is very heavy, dig in some sand or light gravel.

Dig over and prepare the ground as early as possible, and incorporate some well-rotted manure or organic fertilizer. Remove any perennial weeds and rake to a fine tilth. Sow seed in early spring in shallow drills about 23 to 30cm (9 to 12in) apart. The seeds are notoriously slow to germinate. When the seedlings are large enough to handle, around 5cm (2in) in height, they will need thinning. Choose a wet day or water the ground well first if it's dry. Gently pull out seedlings leaving about 15cm (6in) of space for each plant. The thinned-out plants can be transplanted to another bed. Water in well after transplanting. Keep the soil damp and remove weeds by hand as they appear.

Seeds can also be scattered over a prepared bed, but will still need thinning to allow space for the plants to grow. Wait until the plants are large enough to handle before thinning.

savory leaves.

Winter savory from seed

Seed should be treated as summer savory, but check on the seed packet for growing recommendations for your area before sowing. Winter savory is a low-growing shrub and can be positioned at the front of most herb, flower or vegetable beds. It can also be a good border plant.

Winter savory from cuttings

Choose fresh shoots in the summer months and cut just below a 'heel' in the stem. Plant in a seedbed or in pots of fresh compost. Keep soil fairly damp but not too wet, and remove any weeds as they come up. When the cuttings have developed roots they can be re-planted in the garden. Cuttings can be encouraged to produce roots faster by keeping them protected in a greenhouse, but they will normally be fine if planted directly outside. Plant more cuttings than you need to allow for those that don't take.

Winter savory from root division

Dig up a well-established plant in the spring and pull the root apart into several pieces. Re-plant pieces immediately in prepared soil.

Use savory as soon as the plants are growing well and are a few inches tall. Take just a few leaves from each plant until they are well established. As mentioned above, winter savory can get woody and straggly after two or three years and may need replacing.

Storing

Summer or winter savory can be used fresh for most of the year. Winter savory should produce foliage through part of the winter, depending on the severity of the temperatures and the amount of rainfall. Summer savory should be pulled up when the plant is in flower and the whole plant hung upside down in bags in a dark and airy place until dry.

Medicinal uses for savory

Because savory is a warming herb, it has often been used to aid digestion and reduce flatulence. It is also an effective expectorant for relieving coughs and bronchial disorders. Fresh leaves soothe wasp and bee stings.

SORREL (*Rumex acetosa*;
French sorrel – *Rumex scutatus*)
(perennial)

About sorrel

There was mention of sorrel in culinary manuscripts from over 2,000 years ago, but sorrel hasn't been well documented over the centuries, probably because it grows wild and never needed to be cultivated. It is native to Europe and Asia but has spread across America and is now a fairly common garden plant in many countries. Sorrel is in the same family as dock and has been used along with dock for many centuries. Sorrel has survived the taste test of time and is used in many recipes, culinary and medicinal. Dock is rarely used in food preparations nowadays and French sorrel (Rumex scutatus) seems to be the most popular type of sorrel to grow in herb gardens.

Sorrel has similar qualities to spinach and can be prepared and eaten in the same way. However, these plants are poisonous in excess and should be taken in moderation especially by those with liver or kidney complaints.

French sorrel, as the name suggests, is used in many French recipes as well as being a popular 'pot herb'. Both types of sorrel, *Rumex acetosa* and *Rumex scutatus* (French sorrel), are used medicinally as well as in the kitchen.

The plant can grow to around 1.2 to 1.5m (4 to 5ft) in height and produces flowers throughout the summer months.

Properties

The properties of sorrel are very similar to those of dock. Sorrel leaves also have a measurable amount of potassium and vitamin A.

100g raw dock leaves

Vitamin C	Calcium	Iron	Calories
48.0mg	44mg	2.40mg	22

Growing

Sorrel can be grown as an annual or a perennial. After a few years the plants can become coarse and

Sorrel leaf.

should be replaced. Sorrel can be grown in full su and does thrive in a sunny spot, but tends to bolt run to seed quickly in hot dry spells. Either prote your plants from full sun, especially in the hotte part of the day, or plant in a position that will g some shade. Sorrel can be propagated from see or root division.

From seed

Seed can be sown directly in the garden from la spring to early summer. Dig over the bed qui deeply, and remove any perennial weeds. Rake to a fine tilth and sow seeds about 2.5cm (1in) deep in rows around 25 cm (18in) apart. Keep watered but not too wet. When the seedlings are large enough to handle, thin to allow the stronger plants space to grow – that is, approximately 25 to 30cm (10 to 12in). Because sorrel grows in clumps, a spacing of around 30cm (12in) is usually recommended, but if the soil is dug deeply or you are using a raised-bed system sorrel can be grown closer together.

Seeds can also be started early in the year in a greenhouse or conservatory. Sow as early as March, as long as the pots can be kept warm. Sow a few seeds in pots of fresh compost. Make sure the pots are well drained but not allowed to dry out.

It's a good idea to use degradable pots to avoid damaging roots when transplanting to the garden.

After all danger of frost has passed transplant the sorrel plants out into their permanent position in the herb garden or in containers.

Root division

In the autumn, choose a healthy plant and dig up carefully to avoid damaging the roots. Divide the root clump into pieces and re-plant in the garden as soon as possible after digging up. Only plant out pieces of root that are free from disease and healthy. Water in well after planting.

After a few years, sorrel can get coarse and should be replaced as necessary. Sorrel is often grown as an annual from seed every year.

If your sorrel plants start running to seed too early, cut off the flowering stems. The flower stems can be cut off as they appear unless you want to grow the flowers to use, or to allow the plant to seed itself. If left to its own devices sorrel can be somewhat invasive in the herb bed, so keep an eye out for plants coming up everywhere. Sorrel sometimes sends out runners to make new plants. Remove these if you need to contain your sorrel bed. Cut runners from the main plant and dig up the new plants carefully to avoid damaging the roots. Re-plant as soon as possible after digging up.

When the plants start to grow tall in the summer, cut the stems down and the roots will push up fresh new shoots.

Sorrel can be grown in pots.

Storing

Young leaves are best used fresh, but can be dried for use in the winter months, or when the plant is resting. Leaves should be dried on racks or hung in small bunches in a dry and airy place until crisp. Crumble and store in glass jars, then label.

Medicinal uses for sorrel

Sorrel contains high levels of oxalic acid and shouldn't be used in medicinal preparations for people suffering from rheumatism. Sorrel has been used in infusions to treat sore throats and is a 'cooling' herb. It is a natural laxative and is often used to treat constipation. Sorrel is believed to cleanse and purify the body of toxins.

TARRAGON (*Artemisia dracunculus*) (perennial)

About tarragon

Although tarragon is a perennial plant, in cooler climates it is unlikely to produce seed unless it is kept in a warm environment throughout the winter months. The plant will keep growing but will need dividing every two or three years, or fresh seed should be sown regularly to ensure a healthy crop.

In some countries there are restrictions on growing plants of the *Artemisia* family, as well as restrictions on some of the extracts from these plants.

The true French tarragon isn't always easy t[o] grow from seed and the seed is often hard to fin[d] although small plants may be available from goo[d] garden suppliers and nurseries. Russian tarragon [is] slightly coarser but hardier and is often grown i[n] place of French tarragon.

Tarragon can be grown successfully in contain[n]ers but it isn't a particularly decorative plant. It [is] used extensively in cooking as well as being adde[d] to vinegars and salad dressings. It has a subtle fla[vour] vour and is often used to enhance dishes with [a] light flavour. Tarragon is a warming herb and [is] said to stimulate appetite and lower fevers.

Tarragon plant.

The herb is native to southern Europe and is now widely grown throughout Europe and elsewhere.

Properties

1 tbsp fresh leaves (1.8g)

Vitamin C	Calcium	Iron	Calories
0.9mg	21mg	0.58mg	5

Growing

Tarragon can be started from seed, although it is unusual to find true French Tarragon seed. Buy a ready-grown plant from a nursery if the seed is unavailable, or find someone who is growing French tarragon and who would share a cutting or part of a root. Many gardeners find they have too many plants when it comes to perennials, and will happily give some away.

Otherwise, Russian tarragon can be grown from seed and will self-seed in warmer climates, or if protected through cold winter months. Russian tarragon can be propagated by root division as well as the French variety, and should be lifted every few years and divided to give the plants a better chance of thriving.

From seed

Seed is generally sown around April, but check on your seed packet for the manufacturer's growing recommendations. Sow the seed in well-drained trays or pots of fresh compost and keep out of direct light and indoors. Keep trays and pots indoors until the seedlings start to appear. The compost should be kept damp, but not too wet.

When the seedlings are starting to show, the trays can be put outside during the day until the air temperature gets a little warmer. Bring indoors at night. When they are large enough to handle, plant out in their permanent positions. Tarragon grows well in containers although the perennial plants will need replacing every two or three years.

Position your plants in the herb garden or in containers, in a sunny position if possible, although tarragon will also grow well in partial shade. Dig the ground over before planting, and remove any perennial weeds and non-organic debris. Rake to a fine tilth and water plants straight after planting.

Keep weeds away and the ground fairly damp but not too wet.

From cuttings

This is probably the best way to get French tarragon going in your herb garden. Take 8 to 10cm (3 to 4in) cuttings from established plants in the spring and push the cut end of the stems into pots of fresh compost. If you have space in the seedbed, tarragon cuttings can be planted directly outside although they should be protected at night with a cloche during the winter months. Keep watered during dry weather and plant out the following year when the cuttings have developed roots. Both Russian and French tarragon can be propagated from cuttings.

Tarragon leaves.

Root division

Roots can be divided in the spring or autumn. Choose a well-established and healthy plant and dig up carefully to avoid damaging the roots. Divide the root system into a number of pieces and re-plant straight away in a sunny or semi-shade position. Water well, and keep weeds away. Resist picking leaves until the new plants have started growing again.

All tarragon plants have rather straggly root systems and will need to be divided every few years to keep them healthy and thriving. To get the best possible harvest, tarragon is best grown fresh every couple of years, and old plants removed and composted.

Storing

Tarragon is best used fresh, and some varieties are evergreen so the leaves should be available all year round. However, sprigs of tarragon can be frozen. Pick them in the summer when the plant is at its peak, and freeze them quickly. Leaves can also be dried by laying them on trays or hanging them in bunches in a dry, airy place out of direct light. When leaves are fully dry, store in glass jars and label. Keep all dried herbs out of direct light to reduce loss of flavour.

Medicinal uses for tarragon

Tarragon isn't used in medicinal preparations these days although it was once used to treat toothache. However, it is a warming herb and can help reduce fevers. Tarragon also encourages appetite, but is predominantly a culinary herb.

VIOLETS (*Viola odorata*)
(perennial)

About violets

Viola odorata is the species known as sweet violets. The smell and taste of the plant live up to their reputation. Sweet violet flowers are candied and used in many cakes and other confections – they have a unique smell and taste and can't be forgotten once tried. Violets have been used since at least 500BC as a medicinal herb. Both the leaves and the flowers are edible.

Violets are a woodland plant and if left to grow make excellent ground cover, growing to around 8 to 10cm (3 or 4in) in height. The leaves are usable all year round and can be used to thicken stews and added to salads. The delicate flowers normally bloom in late winter and early spring making it one of the first colourful plants in the year. Violet flowers have a very delicate yet unmistakeable scent and can be used in confectionery and also infused in a tisane.

Violets belong to the *viola* family, in which there are hundreds of types, although it is the *viola odorata* (sweet violet) that is most commonly used as a herb. The plants will grow in sunny positions as they are quite hardy and adaptable, but the ground must be kept watered in dry periods. They are happiest in semi-shade and are often found growing wild in light woodland areas.

Properties

Violet plants have astringent properties and can be used as a medicinal or culinary herb. Salicyclic acid is also present in the plant, and this is used in the making of aspirin.

Growing

Violets are best propagated from already established plants. They develop new plants from the roots but they can also be started from seed. Violet flowers are perfect for visiting bees but usually bloom before the bees are out and about, so aren't often pollinated and rarely produce seed. Violets flower again sometimes in autumn but the flower although full of seed, isn't attractive to bees at that time so again doesn't get pollinated. Sowing violets from seed can be erratic and it is usually best to propagate by division of the plants, or by detaching small plants from the runners produced from the main plant.

Violets are a woodland plant and will thrive in semi-shade but as long as the ground doesn't dry out, they will be happy to grow in a sunny position.

Violets.

From seed

If you do want to try your hand at propagating sweet violets from seed, start by buying a packet of seeds from a reputable seed company and check on the manufacturer's growing recommendations before you start. Generally the seed should be planted early in the spring and kept in a warm place. Sow in well-drained pots or trays of fresh compost and keep damp but not too wet. Seeds may take some time to germinate. Although violets can tolerate very low temperatures, if starting from seed, they should be kept indoors until the outside temperature is warmer.

When the seedlings are large enough to handle, and all danger of frost has passed, either re-pot or plant outside in their permanent positions. Allow about 30cm (12in) of growing space per plant.

From runners

In spring or autumn, cut the runner from the main plant and transplant to its new position, in full sun or partial shade. Water plants in well after transplanting, and firm down with your heel.

Root division

In the autumn, plants can be gently lifted and divided into two or more pieces. Dig carefully around the plants to avoid damaging the roots, then re-plant the undamaged and healthy pieces. Plant out in pots or containers, and transplant into the garden during the following spring or autumn, when they are growing well.

Cuttings

Violets can also be started from cuttings taken from healthy plants in the autumn. Push cuttings into well-drained pots of fresh compost, then water them. Look after them during the winter months and plant out the following autumn when the cuttings have developed roots and are starting to grow.

Violet plants are evergreen and the leaves can be used all year round. Young leaves are best used in salads and the larger leaves, produced later in the year, are good to add to soups and stews to thicken them.

The flowers should be picked and used as available. Add to salads or use to flavour sweet dishes. Flowers are often candied and used as decoration for fancy cakes.

Storing

Leaves are evergreen and shouldn't need storing, but can be dried if necessary. Dry by hanging in small bunches in a dark, airy place until crisp, then crumble into glass jars and label. Flowers can be dried for making tea, and also candied for decorating cakes and desserts.

Violet flowers.

Medicinal uses for violets

Many conditions have been treated with violets. In recent years, fresh leaves have been found to be helpful in curing some cancers. The leaves have expectorant properties making it good for alleviating bronchial conditions. It is also a mild laxative and should not be taken in large doses. Violets are used in herbal preparations worldwide, and have been for many centuries.

WATERCRESS (*Nasturtium officinale*) (perennial)

About watercress

Watercress is one of the few herbs you can grow that really does like to be waterlogged. Traditionally grown in streams of running water, watercress can often be found growing wild, although care should be taken when collecting it. The water source could be contaminated with animal drop-

pings or agricultural chemicals that may not affect the taste of the plant but it will affect its properties and cause illness.

Watercress has been used as a medicinal and culinary herb for over 2,000 years and has been considered to be a super food for almost as long. It became a commercial product in the early nineteenth century. By the early twentieth century watercress had developed into large business with London being the heart of the watercress-trading world.

For many years it has been used to encourage growth in children and keep soldiers strong and prepared for battle. As the herb contains, gram for gram, as much vitamin C as oranges; as much calcium as milk; and also vast quantities of potassium and iron, the folklore about watercress being a super food is very likely to be true. There are so many minerals and vitamins in watercress, that eating a bunch a day would probably cancel any need for vitamin supplements.

The herb originated in Europe and Asia but is now grown widely in many countries.

Properties

10 sprigs of raw watercress (25g)

Vitamin C	Calcium	Iron	Calories
10.8mg	30mg	0.05mg	3

Growing

It has, until recently, been thought impossible to grow watercress without a pure spring water source. However, it can be grown in an old paddling pool if conditions are good. If you do happen to have a source of pure spring water, so much the better.

From seed

If you want to grow cress in a regular vegetable bed, you will need to buy seeds of a land cress variety. Check on the packet for manufacturer's growing instructions before you buy. There are a number of ways to get cress going and seed is readily available from garden suppliers. Watercress isn't a true water plant as the plant grows above water and has only

Watercress.

its roots beneath the surface. Seed can be sown in a seed tray of very moist compost but the tray or pot should be well drained and watered regularly. The seed won't germinate in dry conditions, or in stagnant water.

When the plants are large enough to handle plant them out in their permanent position.

If watercress gets well established in your garden, it can become invasive, but harvesting regularly should help overcome this. If left to grow, watercress can grow to about 1m (over 3ft) in length, but shoots are normally cut at around 20cm (8in) or so.

Plants can be placed in a clean and cool garden pond, but the pond must be cleaned regularly or have a running water source pumped through it. Watercress will also survive on the banks of a stream if moist enough. It is also not a particular sun lover and will do well in very cool water and partial shade.

Watercress can be grown at home in an old paddling pool, full of soil. Make sure the pool is well drained and watered regularly. Containers must be well drained so that the water doesn't become stagnant. Watercress ideally thrives in pure spring water.

From cuttings

If you buy your watercress from your greengrocer in bunches they will sometimes take root. Place a few healthy stems in a glass of water and change

Watercress can be kept fresh in water.

the water often. Many of the cuttings will develop roots, which can be planted out later. Or beg a few plants or cuttings from a local grower. Never let the roots dry out, keep the water clean and you should be able to produce a steady crop of this wonderful plant all year round. In the winter months watercress is coarser but can be added to soups and stews, instead of eaten raw in salads.

Harvest watercress often and cut stems that are straggly. When you cut watercress, the roots develop more shoots and the plants become stronger so don't forget to use it.

Read the growing recommendations on seed packets before you buy, as this is a plant that requires out-of-the-ordinary cultivation techniques, and you may have to choose a specific variety for your region and available space.

Storing

Watercress can be stored in a glass of water in a cold place, preferably a fridge, for a couple of days. Place cut end down in an inch or two of fresh cold water. As watercress will often produce fresh shoots all year round, it's not usually necessary to store it.

Medicinal uses for watercress

Watercress has been used to treat many illnesses and medical conditions, too numerable to men-

tion. Because of its very high vitamin and mineral content, including folic acid, which is relatively scarce in plant life, watercress is a natural tonic and will help the body to repair itself. Eating a couple of handfuls of watercress everyday will give the immune system a boost and help stave off colds and flu.

YARROW (*Achillea millefolium*) (perennial)

About yarrow

Yarrow has long been associated with divination and can be found in the *I Ching* or *Book of Changes*. It also has a long medicinal history and has been considered to be one of the most effective healing herbs for centuries. The common name, woundwort, confirms that the herb was used to heal wounds and has been used for stemming nose bleeds and for treating more serious wounds.

Yarrow has been used in culinary and cosmetic preparations as well as being an effective medicinal herb. It can also be used as a substitute for hops in brewing beer.

Yarrow is still used today in home preparations and, in ayurvedic medicine, often employed as a tonic. Prolonged use, however, can cause allergic reactions.

Yarrow is native to Europe but is now fairly widespread over moderate climates, and grows wild in meadows, pastureland and along the roadside. It will always be found growing in a sunny position and often in fairly poor soil.

Cultivating yarrow in the herb garden has to be carefully controlled, as this plant can become invasive. Yarrow is a useful herb for repelling beetles and ants and a plant or two in the vegetable garden will help repel pests. A yarrow plant in a container near the entrance to a house will repel flies.

Properties

The volatile oils and other constituents, including gum, gives this plant wound-healing qualities. It is also considered to be a nutritious herb.

...rrow in flower.

...rowing

...n't plant yarrow in a richly composted area of the ...rden. It doesn't thrive in rich soil and will often ... much better in fairly poor soil conditions as long ... it is in full sun. Yarrow can grow up to 60cm ...4in) tall and needs a sunny position grow well. It ...n be planted alongside pathways where the soil ...sn't been cultivated, or next to the back door to ...pel flies and bugs from entering the house. It can ... propagated from seed or by division.

...Yarrow is very suitable for container growing as it ...lerates drying out occasionally and won't become ...vasive in the garden.

...rom seed

...rrow likes a light soil and a sunny position. If your ...il is too heavy, dig in some sand or light gravel ... add drainage. Plant seed in the spring in well-...ained trays or pots of fresh compost. Or yarrow can ... planted directly in a seedbed and protected from ...ld nights with a cloche, or sow in a cold frame.

...In some regions and with some varieties, seed ...n be planted in the autumn. Check on the manu-facturer's growing recommendations on your seed packet before you sow.

Water the seeds but never let the soil become waterlogged or too wet. The seed can take up to three months to germinate. When the seedlings are large enough to handle they can be pricked out into individual pots or, if the ground and air temperature is warm enough, planted directly out into the garden. Although yarrow is a hardy plant and fairly frost-tolerant, the seedlings will need protecting against bad weather until they are established.

Root division

In the autumn, plants can be divided if necessary. Using a fork, dig carefully around a well-estab-lished healthy plant, and divide into two or more pieces depending on the size of the root structure. Re-plant the divided pieces straight away and heel down. Water in well, and mulch in the winter if the ground is likely to become frozen. Yarrow doesn't like too much moisture so be careful not to mulch too heavily. Plants should not be mulched if the ground is very wet.

From cuttings

Yarrow can also be started from cuttings taken in spring or autumn. Push cuttings 8 to 10cm (3 to 4in) into pots of fresh compost and water. Keep in a sunny spot and water fairly regularly. Always position yarrow in a well-drained and sunny place.

Harvest flowers and leaves as they become available. Young leaves can be added to salads although they are rather bitter to taste. Flowers are often made into tisanes. Be careful yarrow doesn't take over. You may have to pull out a few plants every year to allow the other plants in the garden to breathe. However, if you harvest all the flowers, they won't have a chance to re-seed.

Storing

Leaves and flowers can be dried. Hang stems upside down in paper bags in a dark and airy place until completely dry. The whole herb, leaves and fl[ow]ers, can be used to make tea as well as in medic[al] preparations. The flowers also make a nice d[ried] flower arrangement.

Medicinal uses for yarrow

A compress can be made from yarrow to assist healing of wounds. Tea made from fresh leav[es] often successful in alleviating cold and flu sy[mp]toms. Yarrow has been used in many medic[al] aids for centuries. It is still used today in he[rbal] remedies treating kidney disorders, menstrual [pain] and other conditions. However, taken regu[larly] over a long period of time it can be harmful. A s[prig] of yarrow thrown onto the barbecue after coo[king] will repel mosquitoes.

Yarrow leaves.

cknowledgements

any thanks to Emily Barker and Lucy Gray for
e bulk of the photographs in this book. Also,
nk you to the following for their individual
otographic contributions: Anna Kirsten Dickie
age 9); D. McAbee (pages 9, 83 and 119); Kevin
sseel (page 13); Clara Natoli (page 21); Jane M.
wyer (page 23); Sheba Duh Kitty (page 30);
er (page 41); Xenia Antunes (page 48); Destiny
Cole (page 56); Mary R. Vogt (pages 65 and 120);
Saffy (page 66); Gracey Stinson (page 69); Eugenia
Beecher (page 87); R. S. Harts (page 88); George
M. Bosela (page 101); Rachel (page 102); Frank
(page 105); Derek Benjamin Lilly (page 106);
Malinda Welte (page 123); Steven L. Berg (page
108); and Rhoda Nottridge (frontispiece, pages 6,
8, 20, 32, 37, 39, 42, 47, 61, 73 and 91).

Further information

FURTHER READING

Bown, Deni, *The Royal Horticultural Society Encyclopaedia of Herbs and Their Uses* (Dorling Kindersley, 2003)

Castleman, Michael, *The New Healing Herbs* (Hinkler Books, 2003)

Gray, Linda, *Granny's Book of Good Old Fashioned Common Sense* (Black & White Publishing, 2007)

Gray, Linda, *Grow Your Own Pharmacy* (Findhorn Press, 2007)

Stuart, Malcolm, *The Encyclopaedia of Herbs and Herbalism* (Caxton, 1989)

WEBSITES

BBC Gardening: www.bbc.co.uk/gardening

Botanical: www.botanical.com

Flower and Garden: www.flower-and-garden-tips.com

National Gardening Association: www.garden.org

Index